"Inside every one of us is a Little Dog and a Big Dog. Those who master the mental techniques of controlling their Dogs, are the ones who leave the field victorious."

— Steve Knight

Library of Congress Catalog Control Number: 2004195783
Publisher's Cataloging-in-Publication
(Prepared by Let's Win! Publishing).

Let's Win! Publishing
1511 SW Park Avenue #812
Portland, OR 97201

WinningSTATE-BOYS' SOCCER: Program Your Mind—Win The Confidence Battle.
/ by Steve Knight—1st ed.

   p. cm.
ISBN: 0-9765361-3-7

1. Sports 2. Soccer 3. Psychology
l. Knight, Steve ll. Title.

9 8 7 6 5 4 3 2

PRINTED IN THE UNITED STATES OF AMERICA

Winning
STATE™
Soccer

Program Your Mind
Win The Confidence Battle

STEVE KNIGHT

Let's Win!
Publishing

CONTENTS

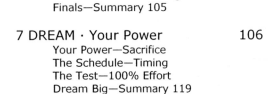

WinningSTATE-SOCCER

PREFACE

I entered my first weightlifting tournament in 1974. I barely knew how to perform the lifts, and I knew nothing about the *process* of a tournament—I was totally in the dark about competing. My only previous sports experience had been Little League baseball.

I placed last, but survived the inaugural tournament, and went on to spend eleven years as a competitive weightlifter. I won several state and two national championships; in 1982 I set an Oregon state record in the Squat of 722 lbs, which still stands today. I lifted in the 181 lb weight class.

While conducting numerous seminars on competing and strength training across the country, I am invariably asked how I mentally prepared for the big lifts, and how I kept it mentally together at the big tournaments. Those are hard questions to meaningfully answer in a seminar setting, and there aren't very many books or videos about preparing mentally for competition to recommend.

Due to that lack of resources and remembering my own confusion during the pre-national (rookie) years, I often wondered how a book on developing the mental skills of a competitor would be received.

In the fall of 2001, I decided to write *WinningSTATE-Wrestling*, a how-to book on focusing the competitive mind and systematically constructing a *game mindset*. My core objective was to help wrestlers better understand the mental side of competing, so they could perform well under pressure. My objective quickly evolved into helping athletes in all sports, program their minds, conquer doubt, and better manage the game environment—to become the "complete" athlete.

WinningSTATE confidence books (Baseball, Basketball, Football, and Wrestling) have been so well received, I decided to adapt my confidence building techniques and distractions management routines specifically for soccer players.

Here's to the Big Dog deep inside us all.

Let's Win!

ACKNOWLEDGEMENTS

As I look back over months of preparation, many individuals come to mind who influenced the outcome of WinningSTATE-SOCCER.

But, before I make special mention of a few impact players, I must, with tremendous gratitude, thank the coaches and players who appear in the "Interviews w/Champions" section. I sincerely appreciate all of your efforts. Thank you!

To the moms and dads of the players profiled—thank you very much for your efforts.

To ALL the photographers: your photos make this book come alive. Thank you.

To Michelle Murphy-Terry at Western Oregon University and the team in Academic Advising: Thanks for sharing the "Inspirational Quotes" you assembled.

To Ken Kelly: Your art is incredible. www.kenkellyart.com

To Paul Riley and the University of Indiana Athletics: Thanks for giving us permission to use that great image on the cover.

To Layne Ross: Thanks for your simple advice, "If it ain't broke, don't fix it." Thanks for putting yourself at risk, and we all are very happy you (and your brother) made it home safe!

To Nick Bahr: Fantastic job with the website, 5-minute movie, promotion, photos, and interviews. You've developed into a solid, trusted co-worker. Thanks very much for your consistency and creative involvement. Level 3 soon.

To my friend Kim Ross: Your initial encouragement was invaluable. Thanks so much for your many hours, your energy, and your genuine interest in this project.

Finally, to Jody, Dan, and Sam: Yeah baby—she's on the move! Thanks … always … for your love and caring.

DEDICATION

To my first coach: Honestly, I don't think I would have made it through those confusing, difficult, adolescent years without your influence, direction, and unselfish involvement. Many of the concepts you shared and taught are at the core of this book.

Forever, you will be at the top of my impact list.

This is for you.

"Steve Knight is one of the few American Powerlifters who displays the mental control and confidence of the European Olympic Lifters."

Bill Starr, Author
Defying Gravity—How To Win At Weightlifting

INTRODUCTION

WinningSTATE Confidence Books are the first of their kind; the first books to break down in simple form the mental side of competing. Within these chapters you'll learn to focus your mind, and believe in your physical abilities; you'll learn to successfully battle the natural ups-and-downs of insecurity and self-doubt; ultimately, you'll develop the confidence and composure of a veteran competitor.

I've attended hundreds of sporting events over my thirty-year athletic career, and what never ceases to amaze me is the number of athletes who suffer defeat because they aren't prepared mentally .

I've seen distracted, fearful minds—coupled with disorganized approaches to games and tournaments—leave thousands of great athletes sitting in dejection and bewilderment after losing a major competition that they should have won. To win games, to be a champion at any level, an athlete needs two sets of skills: the physical skills of his sport, and the mental skills of a competitor. This is why I've written *WinningSTATE Confidence Books*.

The world-class techniques, methods, and routines I present can be applied to all sports, but this edition of *WinningSTATE* is specifically for soccer players of all ages who want to take their competitive skills to a winning level.

As a former state and national Powerlifting champion I'm familiar with hard work, but playing soccer, no matter the position, requires a physical skill-set that is way beyond hard work; it requires quick judgment, hand-eye coordination, and extraordinary split-second timing. Then, in a game setting, add intense pressure to win, a packed stadium, and heightened emotions to make the key pass, the big penalty shot, or scoring the winning goal, and the need for having the mental skills of a seasoned competitor becomes crystal clear.

I've watched countless stud athletes over the years endure the commitment to practice that is required for high-level sports, only to go to games and fall apart (or "lay-an-egg" as a friend of mine would say). All too often, great soccer players crumble mentally and lose long before they ever set foot on the field—I call this a *confidence meltdown*.

INTRODUCTION CON'T

A meltdown is painful to watch because these same dazed, doubt-dominated players would be fearless, if they had a second set of skills: *the mental skills of a competitor.*

Let me ask you, what's the point of developing high-level physical skills, if mentally you're a weak competitor? It's pointless, unless practice is the only reason you're out for the sport, which I doubt is the case for most of you; most of you want to compete, and win!

My passion for writing this book is to help soccer players of all ages find their Big Dog that lives deep inside. My hope is that *WinningSTATE-SOCCER* will not only be visually entertaining and competitively inspiring, but also a powerful competitive tool for players, coaches, and parents alike. My goal is to help players become champions, and to help rookies make their first "clutch" play.

As competitors, other than winning, the most gratifying feeling is knowing that as we faced the pressure we didn't flinch. Win or lose, we know we rose to the occasion and competed. Win or lose, when the final second is over, we're able say to ourselves truthfully: "I didn't choke. I gave it all I had."

I encourage you to study the techniques and routines in the following chapters to take your competitive skills to the next level, find your Big Dog deep inside and *believe in yourself,* so you can deliver the level of play you're capable of—"clutch" game winning play.

Here's to believing,

Steve Knight
Author
WinningSTATE Confidence Books

Winning
STATE™
Soccer

Let's Win!
Publishing

Chapter 1

WINNING • A Game Mindset

You know how to play the game. You've worked hard at practice. Your skills are sharp, you know how to attack the ball, and you're an aggressive tackler. You're strong, you're conditioned, and you know what you're capable of. You've dreamed about blowing past your opponent to make that perfect pass or kick the winning goal. But instead, when the pressure is on, you doubt yourself, miss the key play or give the ball up. Too many times you've ended up walking off the field feeling disappointed and dejected, knowing you could've played a better game; you wonder why you didn't have your best game when you needed it the most. You wonder what's missing. You wonder why the last game of the season has never been your best. You wonder what will take your confidence to the next level. Answer: It's time to learn how to compete—*mentally*.

"We are what we repeatedly do.
Excellence, then, is not an act,
but a habit."
— Aristotle

Above: Gardner-Webb's men's soccer team took a 2-1 win over Georgia State when Brian Young scored the second goal of the game with a bicycle kick. Photo by Bob Carey

Left: Thousand Oaks High soccer players, from left, Kenny Negron, Jason Leopoldo and Erick Alvarez celebrate their CIF 1-0 victory over Loyola. Photo by Joseph A. Garcia/Star Staff

Games are entirely unlike practice. The excitement, the strange environment, the players you've never faced before, freaked-out teammates and the tremendous pressure to win all require **mental skills** which must be developed, just like dribbling, passing, and shooting. Physically, most athletes train their butts off, but mentally they do very little to prepare for competition. *WinningSTATE—SOCCER* focuses on the mental skills clutch players use in pressure situations to perform consistently at a high-level.

WinningSTATE—SOCCER explains the fundamentals of thinking like a competitor. I talk about what drives a champion, the difference between practice and competition, and how to mentally approach games ready to compete. I outline how to develop a *focused game mindset,* which will take your competitive skills to the next level and will instantly improve your game performance—*guaranteed.*

"One important key to success is self-confidence. An important key to self-confidence is preparation."

— Arthur Ashe

Above: D2 Men's Soccer National Champion Seawolves. Photographer unknown.

Left: Ruiz trips up Colorado's Kyle Beckerman. Photo by Essy Ghavameddini/MLS/WireImage

The Stadium: Conquer It

Being in an unfamiliar stadium, in an unfamiliar city, with huge crowds, and all kinds of distractions can be overwhelming to say the least. It can shatter your concentration if you don't have solid mental plan.

Chapter 2 will show you how to effectively deal with the intensity of the stadium environment. You will learn an important mental technique: How to narrow your thinking to only the Battle Zones, the four physical locations in every stadium where all of the action takes place. Chapter 2 will also teach you seven primary Confidence Routines for maintaining perfect focus in pressure situations. Combined, these techniques and routines will bring the typically unpredictable, chaotic stadium environment under control. You'll learn how to ignore distractions, stay focused, and ultimately to *conquer the Stadium*.

"By developing a Game Mode mindset you'll take your competitive skills to the next level."

Nutrition: Game Fuel

Nutrition is often an undervalued component of non weight-cutting sports. If your goal is to be a consistent pressure player, especially during the big games, *nutrition cannot be ignored.* To compete on a superior level our bodies need clean-burning, high-octane, quick-recovery fuel: fresh fruits, grains, and good fats—not weak, low-energy tongue food: candy, plastic cheese, hot dogs, and colored sugar water, just to name a few.

Chapter 3 won't show you how to eat to please your tongue; it will show how to fuel-up for optimum 2nd half performances.

Attitude: Game Mode

Attitude makes champions – not perfect physical skills or intimidating physical size. Attitude is the glue that brings all of the physical and mental training together. As competitors *we live or die by attitude.*

Inside every one of us are a Little Dog and a Big Dog. Different factors make some of us more Little Dog than BIG: personality type, genetic make-up, and environmental factors. But mostly it's genetic—some puppies bite, and some puppies don't. The question is: Can passive puppies learn to be aggressive dogs?

Chapter 4 will help you understand where you naturally fit on the Dog Scale, but most importantly, Little Dogs will learn how to let their Big Dog out, and Big Dogs will learn how to calm themselves down.

You learn that Game Mode is about being serious, not acting serious. It's about pure attitude. It's about leaving your real life in the parking lot and stepping into a competitive frame of mind. Game Mode is about developing the mental perspective that transforms passive puppies into aggressive dogs. It's about developing a second set of skills, the mental skills of a competitor. Game Mode is about stepping-up with confidence and competing to win.

Above: St. Ignatius defender Adam Danko celebrates the Wildcats' lone goal in a victory over Westerville North. Photo by Gus Chan/Plain Dealer

Big Dog Visualization

Next to nutrition, visualization is the most misunderstood component of high-level competition. Typically, visualization is thought of as "seeing" victory. Seeing yourself making great defensive plays or kicking the winning goal. Let me ask you: How is seeing victory going to prevent you from wetting yourself when you're banging shoulders with a fire-breathing opponent? Answer: It can't.

Chapter 5 will teach you a new "replacement" visualization technique: Big Dog Visualization. You'll learn how to conquer doubt by finding your true competitive confidence, which will help you compete at a higher level, not just stroke your ego by fantasizing over a fictitious victory celebration. Big Dog Visualization is what will help you transform doubt into confidence, so you can deliver the level of play you're capable of—clutch, game winning play.

"The battle that will make you a champion is fought in your mind, not on the field."

Above: When your opponent seems like a monster is when mental confidence skills are needed most.   Poster: "Looming Menace." Artist: Ken Kelly.   Go to www.kenkellyart.com

Left: 2003 NCAA Championships IU vs. Saint Johns. Photo by Paul B. Riley/IU Athletics

The Battle: Composure

The battle that will make you a champion is fought in your mind, not on the field. The battle is between doubtful or confident. As the game progresses toward the pressure moments, emotions surge. As you battle for position late in the second half, your stomach twists. This is the critical time for many of you. It's when your Little Dog takes over; you crash and burn mentally, right at that pivotal point when it's time to step-up and deliver.

Chapter 6 will teach you how to *show some teeth*; how to stay emotionally balanced and confident during pressure situations, so your Big Dog can come out and dominate. You'll see your opponent through your Big Dog "I can" mindset, so you can take control of the rhythm and deliver explosive, attacking play.

Dream: Your Power

Your dream is your power, and it must be crystal clear. When you're hanging with your friends and it's time for drills or mental preparation exercises, why do you head home to practice rather than just keep having fun? When your team is down in the 2nd half and you need to dig down deep to manage the emotional pressure, where does the confidence come from? When you're tempted by friends who are experimenting with dangerous things, who don't care about your eligibility and want you to go along and partake, why do you say, "Nah, I think I'll pass." Answer: You have a dream. The power to discipline yourself, to make tough social decisions comes from your dream, and it must be crystal clear. Do you want to distinguish yourself as a champion, or live among the average?

Chapter 7 will help you clearly define your dream. It will help you understand how your dream is your power, and how your dream provides the motivation to stick with your training, to be the very best you can be—a champion.

Dream big! Create your power.

Above: The keeper's anguish. Photo by Dias dos Reis.

"The world doesn't owe me anything, but it deserves my very best."

— Author Unknown

SUMMARY

- Program your mind to win the confidence battle.

- Mentally separate practice from games.

- Narrow your focus to conquer distractions.

- Think with a Game Mode mindset.

- Find your confidence with Big Dog Visualisation.

- Control your Dogs to stay composed.

- Dream big. Create your power.

"Competing successfully under pressure takes two sets of skills: **Physical skills AND mental skills.** *When you program your mind, as well as work your body, you'll be able to perform at a winning level.*

The key mental skills that transform a doubtful player into a confident competitor are captured in the 7 bullets above. Concentrate and believe."

— Steve Knight

Chapter 2

THE STADIUM • Conquer It

The stadium challenges the *focus* of many young athletes: intense coaches, sideline dynamics, opposing players, and thousands of fans. The distractions are nonstop and the confusion can be overwhelming. The intensity of the stadium can take you out of your comfort zone and leave you numb, babbling in the corner, if you don't have a mental plan.

For many rookies, the immensity of the building, the loud noise, the constant visual distractions and overall game commotion—coupled with extreme emotional instability—make for an unpredictable roller coaster

"The only place success comes before work is in the dictionary."

— Vince Lombardi

Above: LA Galaxy at Colorado Rapids, Invesco Field, Denver CO; imagine playing in front of 10,000 cheering fans. Photo by Jesse Roberge

Left: UVA vs. Long Island U. Soccer. Players unknown. Photo source: pbase.com/waterwagen

experience. Simply put, distractions keep many athletes from achieving their true competitive potential; they haven't developed the mental skills to block out stadium distractions and focus on what's important—their confidence.

Game Mode

If you sacrifice, commit the time, and hard work to compete with the Big Dogs at the "title" tournaments, you must show up mentally dialed-in, ready to get the most out of yourself. Realize that the primary way to deliver consistent, high-level performance in pressure situations is to be mentally focused and composed. Additionally, being able to remain mentally competitive for long hours during games and over several weeks during the playoffs, requires a series of routines which quickly allows you to turn *Game Mode* on and off when you need it most—maximizing concentration and minimizing distractions.

It is vital to make a clear mental distinction: practices are drastically different from games. When competing, everything centers on maximizing your ability to turn your focus on and off at will. Unlike many sports, soccer is not a hurry up and wait situation; while you're in the game—there is very little down time. So having the mental skills to turn Game Mode on and off is a necessity for high-level clutch play.

What specifically is Game Mode? Simply put: It's a very serious mindset. And therein lies the problem. Most young athletes don't know how to be serious, which is why there are more posers than players in sports. A clutch athlete can't "act" serious; he's either serious or he's not. Making faces, grunting, and trying to look all tough is not serious. To most young athletes, serious just means angry or overly emotional. Much of the time, when young athletes get really serious they cry, which is understandable because being serious is emotion, and it's hard to control emotions.

Above: Great soccer fans. Photo source www.texassports.com

Left: Maine's Greg Bajek tries to clear the ball during the game against Harvard University. Photo by Evan Whitney

Serious is about attitude; it's about focused, steely eyed, piercing concentration. No acting, no pretending, no faking, just pure concentration on a specific target. That's serious. That's Game Mode!

Another way to think of Game Mode is having laser beam focus at specific moments, while mentally chilling the rest of the time. Game Mode is being able to turn maximum concentration on in an instant, and turning it off the next. Game Mode is the ability to take your mind to a competitive place, a place very different from most social situations. **Game Mode is about competing to win, not playing for fun.**

Game Mode is about more than wanting to win; it's having the skills to concentrate under pressure, so you can conquer your doubt and then dominate the competition.

Keep this in mind: We win or lose by believing, and believing is about focus and confidence. Focused and confident *is* a Game Mode mindset.

Over many years of competing on a state and national level, I developed seven Confidence Routines that provide mental structure and lay the foundation to be able to turn Game Mode on and off at will: Pack It, Fuel It, Rest It, Analyze It, Visualize It, Compose It and Dominate It.

Unlike emotions, *WinningSTATE* Confidence Routines don't vary from the first minute to the last. They are consistent routines that help create and maintain a focused game mindset, so you can calm your fears, visualize your strengths, and solidify your confidence for crucial plays.

Battle Zones

Now that you have a clearer mental picture of what a Game Mode attitude actually is, and before we get into the nuts-and-bolts of developing your own personal game-time Confidence Routines, first, we need to talk about the Battle Zones—one of the key mental tools for conquering the stadium.

Picture the stadium where your state tournament is held. See the outside, the concessions area, the stripped field, thousands of seats, the scoreboard, the lights, the sounds, the smells ... got the picture?

Now, narrow your focus to just four physical locations in every stadium, the Battle Zones: The Locker Room, The Bench, The Field, and The Win Zone. Every game is mentally controlled from those four physical locations.

Why is narrowing your focus important? Think of a game as if you're walking across a narrow beam high off the ground. What's the first rule? Don't look down. Why? Because looking down will engage your fear, and take your concentration off your balance. You'll stumble, fall, and you're dead.

The stadium presents the same kind of challenge. Engaging the commotion always going on somewhere in the stadium puts you inside the commotion and the commotion inside of you. It's distracting and takes focus away from competing. Our minds can only do one thing at a time; we're either mentally scattered, visually wandering around the stadium in Little Dog poser mode—or we are mentally focused on the game, preparing for battle in Big Dog player mode. Now we're going to breakdown each Battle Zone.

The Locker Room: Before league games, or at the big "title" games, final mental preparations happen in the Locker Room. It's when most of us need to grapple with our competitive minds—both of them—our scared mind and our confident mind. All too often, especially for young athletes away from home, the Locker Room represents time to have fun; this isn't a bad thing, as long as you don't lose perspective—you're there to compete, not fool around.

The Locker Room is a place to collect your self emotionally, make mental confidence adjustments, fuel, rest, and prepare yourself for the game. We'll discuss how to utilize the Locker Room to focus your confidence further in Chapter 4.

The Field: Remember, the objective here is to narrow your thinking so you can focus on your confidence. This Battle Zone (The Field) is not about your position or its requirements; it's about being emotionally comfortable with any field in the country. Why? Because you want to count on being

Battle Zones
Narrow Your Focus

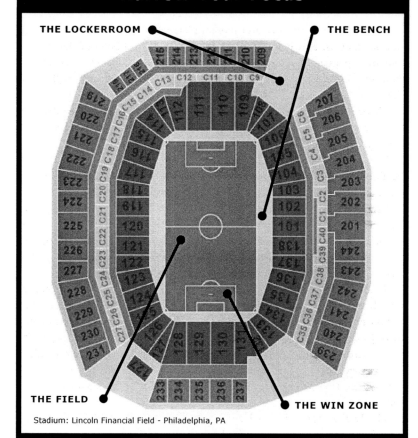

THE LOCKERROOM

THE BENCH

THE FIELD

THE WIN ZONE

Stadium: Lincoln Financial Field - Philadelphia, PA

Narrow your focus to the 4 Battle Zones in every stadium. You'll reduce visual distractions and dramatically increase your ability to deliver focused play.

Winning
STATE™
Soccer

Above: St. Joe's Joseph Mattioli, bottom, sliding tackle strips the ball away from St. Peter's Tom Conigatti. Photo by Hilton Flores/ S.I. Advance

able to be focused and confident wherever you go—no mystery, no drama. A goal is a goal. Yeah, the frame might be a little different—some colored, some not, but basically "goals" are the same. Yes, you'll need to make some visual adjustments the first time you walk onto a new field, but once you compare similarities to your home field, and then adjust your thinking to make the away field your own, you're home—literally. So mentally you can treat any stadium in the country as if you were playing on your own home field.

Before the ref starts the game, everything is happening only in your mind. You can see yourself being a stud, executing like a Big Dog, but then

Confidence
The Player's Guide

7 Steps To Competitive Confidence:

#1   **Battle Zones**
Narrow your focus to 4 physical locations in every stadium—the Battle Zones.

#2   **Game Fuel**
Fuel with high-energy carbs and fats, not weak, low-energy tongue food.

#3   **Get Real**
Grapple with both of your competitive minds. Believe in your Big Dog "I can" psychology.

#4   **Believe**
Focus on previous "stud" performances. Don't think about negative "what if" possibilities.

#5   **Game Mode**
Flip the switch; be able to turn laser beam focus on and off. **Confidence comes from concentration.**

#6   **Big Dog Visualization**
Insert confident DVD—use Big Dog Visualization to transform doubt into confidence. Relive actual memories when you were ... *the Dog.*

#7   **Cowboy-Up**
In every game, at some point, it comes down to proving yourself. Are you a poser or a player? Cowboy-Up!

Program your mind to block out distractions and crush Little Dog doubt to achieve outstanding competitive confidence. *Let your Big Dog out!*

© 2005 Let's Win! Publishing

"The only one who can tell you 'you can't' is you. And you don't have to listen." — Nike

BAM! The next vision is seeing yourself faked out or giving up the ball. Confidence is a constant roller coaster.

The Field is where you use the Doubt Meter to keep close watch on your confidence level. Are you emotionally solid or coming apart? The Field is where most of us flip the switch from chilling to serious. It's where we show some teeth and let our Big Dog out. When we're in the game, it's a constant mental battle to keep our thinking narrow to concentrate on what we want to do, versus what we don't want to do. Remember, Game Mode is about serious, and serious is not about faking, grunting, and faces. Game Mode about focusing on your Big Dog deep inside, and executing your brains out

---

"Game Mode is about focusing on your Big Dog deep inside, and executing your brains out every time."

---

every time. Think about it: if you and your teammates could maintain a Game Mode mindset for an entire game, and throughout the season, you'd be champions.

Just in case this Battle Zone (The Field) needs a little more clarity, bring your focus down to the familiarity of any Field, rather than up and distracted by the immensity of the building—the field is not the building. The field is the field, so look down at the field, not up at the stands—you're there to focus and compete, not mentally wander around the stadium—leave that to the fans. Concentrate on what is directly in front of you on the field, which is familiar, rather than "out there" in the building, which is unfamiliar. Convince your mind that you know The Field, no matter where you're competing. If you practice this mental process there is absolutely no reason to be uncomfortable in a new stadium, because The Field at every stadium is your home Field—you mentally own it.

The Bench: Wow! Bench dynamics. This is one of the fascinating aspects of competing as a soccer player. On the Bench, you're usually sandwiched between teammates, which can make mental preparation difficult. If your teammates are distracted, freaked out, or even worse talking about social BS, they can ruin your Game Mode mindset during any brief substitutions you might get. If you're not a starter it's even worse, because you spend

Above: Union Catholic's Matt Cunha tries to block the kick of Union's Sean Oliveira. Photo by Jim Wright/Star-Ledger

more time on the bench than on the field. Your teammates' unstable mindset can affect you, if you haven't developed a way to narrow your thinking and to concentrate on your confidence instead of getting lost in their lack of confidence. Posers emotionally grab hold of everyone around them because they're scared to death and need reassurance, and it's highly contagious; if you're not careful you'll get sucked into their negative emotional drama.

Those of you who want to deliver clutch play need to have routines that get your mind "right" before you come off the Bench and enter the game. We'll talk more about these mental routines to get your mind "right" in Chapter 4, but for now realize that most of you lose your competitive edge on the Bench, by getting involved with emotional drama and non-game discussions. Rest your mind on the Bench, so you're ready for anything when you're in the game. Remember: The mind of a champion is about discipline, so discipline yourself to focus during certain times and chill during others.

Above: Glencoe-Lakeridge JV Soccer. Players unknown. Photo by John Lariviere

Bench Time: Hardly anyone plays the entire game, so some rest time on the bench is inevitable. Bench Time is especially critical for those of you who play a lot of minutes; you need Bench Time to disconnect and mentally recover. When you're getting that breather...mentally chill as well. Close your eyes for a few seconds, focus your breathing, and calm your emotions. Don't let the distractions of other teammates and fans steal your mental rest period - you need it to recover as much as possible. In the last minutes of the game, being bent over, winded, and ineffective, isn't just from being physically drained; it's also from being mentally drained. If you use your Bench Time wisely - you'll be mentally ready to make that clutch play in the closing minutes.

The Win Zone: We purposefully label the area closest to the goal as the Win Zone, but actually, the Win Zone is anywhere on the field where you and your opponent are battling for position—a small 10' x 10' contact area that surrounds you and your opponent. Whether you're a defender, midfielder, or forward, the Win Zone is where it all happens. During those many one-on-one moments in a game, when you need to be sharp and dangerous, when you need to play with heart and skill, that is when your mind needs to be clearly focused on a particular game situation, not on distractions going on in the stadium.

To be able to deliver clutch play, there can't be any questions about what you're going to do. No matter where you're at on the field, or whatever the game situation might be, you're mental routines have to keep you in a focused, Big Dog frame of mind. The Win Zone is where it all comes together; it's where you accept the challenge of shutting down the opposition's best players, and get the opportunity to take your game to a winning level.

By seeing the stadium as 4 mental Battle Zones, all the important locations of any stadium become familiar. Battle Zones help us deal with our surroundings so that our surroundings won't confuse us in new situations. Now, what's weird is, there are different circumstances surrounding different segments of the game. Sometimes the focus is to keep pressure on the ball, other times you'll need to make that perfect pass, and still other times your team needs a critical goal. But guess what, even though all those circumstances are different and each moment has different requirements and emotional intensity, your execution and mindset stays the same. Bringing your concentration down to the Battle Zones makes all the difference, because you're focused on being in the moment, which enables you to execute, not think about negative "what if" possibilities. What's my point? Getting mentally involved with all the emotional drama of the different game situations is a distraction. Tune into the game and what's required; narrow your thinking to your confidence and superior physical skills, and execute. A confident, attacking, no-hesitation, eyes-open execution will get the job done every time, and the rest will be history.

In summary, narrowing your thinking to the 4 Battle Zones is a psychological technique that helps you manage distractions and emotional drama during games. Learning how to narrow your thinking is one of the key techniques in controlling your mind and emotions: a critical part of *conquering the stadium.*

Confidence Routines

The 7 Confidence Routines are another set of mental tools that will help you conquer the stadium and negative emotions, so you can deliver high-level play. Actually, the 7 Confidence Routines are divided into two pre-game routines and five in-game routines. Follow these routines before and during every game.

Pack It: On game day, especially before you leave for an away game, packing your game necessities is critical. First, make a list—a written list. Then make sure ALL of your necessities are gathered together and ready to be packed: equipment, clothes, food, fluids, accessories, etc. Example: If you want specific clothes along for after the game, list it and pack it. If you have specific music that you use on the bus and in the Locker Room, list it and pack it. Whatever is important to you, list it and pack it.

This may seem trivial, but it's not. For big games you need to make yourself as psychologically comfortable as possible, and your "things" help accomplish that.

Why put out the extra effort to make a list? Because when there are a lot of things to organize and you don't want to leave anything behind, a list provides assurance.

Little Dogs: Your mother is not your list—do it yourself.

Don't pack your bag(s) until you've gathered everything in a group on the floor in front of you and can check it off before you pack it. Be organized and meticulous about packing your necessities. Not only will you have everything you want and need at the game, being organized puts your mind in a calm, focused place—a **Game Mode mindset.**

Fuel It: If you're a junk-food eater and a colored sugar-water drinker,

Above: Players unknown. Photo by MiroFotos: mire-foto.smugmug.com

study Chapter 3 with heightened interest. The Fuel & Hydration Routine is one of the KEY routines to ensuring your competitive advantage.

Rest It: Resting is less for your body and more for your mind and emotions. The psychological intensity of maintaining composure during the final 30 minutes before a big game, and the emotional ups-and-downs during the game itself are very draining, and require constant mental regrouping. To repeat: resting is less for your body and more for your mind and emotions.

Optimally, you want to get *horizontal*, but in soccer, except for a brief period in the locker room before suiting-up or during the halftime break, getting horizontal is impossible, so you have to devise a way to rest sitting up or standing. When you're not on the field, close your eyes briefly and mentally chill. Breathe deep, and calm your mind. You'll be amazed at what 30 seconds of disconnection can do for your recovery, energy level, and competitive focus. Make yourself as comfortable as possible on the bus or in the Locker Room. Your mental freshness will be that much better if you're able to close your eyes and disconnect periodically—even if it's just for a few seconds or minutes.

Analyze It: Clutch play isn't about luck; it's about presence of mind. One of the factors is analyzing the variables of the game so you can make solid decisions. You've studied film, the coaches have put together a solid game plan, but it takes real-time analysis to make it all happen. You're thinking about your strengths and the key plays your team has worked on. Mentally, you must have a routine you automatically use to continuously analyze the variables of the game. This isn't laser beam focus like Game Mode; it's more like being mentally present in the game vs. daydreaming about your girlfriend, or what you and your buddies are doing after the game. The more you stay mentally engaged in analyzing real-time variables, the better your performance will be. Stay mentally in the game as much as possible, except when you're purposefully chilling.

Visualize It: Visualization is one of the most important aspects of high-level performance. I've devoted an entire chapter to teaching you Big Dog Visualization techniques, so read Chapter 5 over and over until you under-stand the process and can visualize your strengths at will. You'll use Big Dog Visualization techniques constantly.

Compose It: Confidence comes and goes; it's fleeting—especially for a young athlete. As pressure situations build or as a critical play approaches, your nerves explode. This is where composure skills are vital. Chapter 6 is your guide to utilizing the mental skills you're building to stay composed during intense pressure situations. You'll learn how to detect an emotional meltdown (when you're coming unglued), and you'll have a routine to keep yourself composed.

Dominate It: This is more of an attitude than a routine. Even though there is a mental sequence to go through, you'll find that dominating is as simple as executing while you're in a Game Mode frame of mind. Being able to dominate is actually a natural result of doing everything else right. Fol-low me? Let's break it down.

If you're practiced and conditioned, if you understand that competing is more than just playing, if you're rested, focused, and composed, and know how to let your Big Dog out, if you truly believe in yourself no matter the situation, and if you can take that mindset and show some teeth as you face the competition, you're automatically in Game Mode and you'll dominate whatever is in front of you.

In summary, by narrowing your focus to the 4 Battle Zones and continu-ously using the 7 Confidence Routines, the stadium and all of its physical and emotional distractions become manageable. They are mental techniques you use to put yourself in position to get the most out of yourself, when it's all on the line.

Stay Focused

Before and during the game there's always something purposeful to do. Oddly enough, chilling is sometimes purposeful. Chilling at certain times requires discipline. It sounds weird, but mentally chilling at critical times makes you a disciplined individual. Why do I point this out? Do the math. During games the amount of unfocused time is far greater than intensely focused time. That's why it's essential to learn the right way to chill. You have to maximize your downtime, so your competitive mind can recover and be ready for each clutch moment.

Guys, as I've stated before, being a true competitor is not about luck or some special mental gift or power, it's about being mentally disciplined - requiring your mind to do what you want it to do, when you want it to do it. Very often during unfocused time, it is vital to just chill.

For a soccer player this can be a bit tricky, because the ball moves from offense to defense in an instant. But, if you're a defender and the forwards are working the ball closer and closer to a scoring position, at that moment the heat is off of you; so purposefully chill for a few seconds. Again, this is a bit complex. I'm not suggesting to disengage from the game, I'm just saying ... BREATHE ... and mentally regroup. If you defenders, or forwards do this each time the ball is at the other end of the field, you'll have more mental energy at the end of the game during those pivotal must stop or score situations. You midfielders don't have quite the same opportunities. You're position is almost constantly engaged, except when the ball is on the opposite side of the field. But, if you pay attention you'll get your opportunities to mentally relax for a few seconds here and there, which is a version of staying focused. Meaning, if you're not focused, how do you know when it's a good time to letdown and chill for a few seconds?

No matter what happens, do your best to stay focused, whether you're in an intense battle or when you're just chilling and thinking about everything you've been doing right, and how you're going to dominate you're opponent during your next encounter.

A Game Mode mindset boils down to a simple perspective: **It's not social!** Everything in real life is put on hold. Everything. Nothing matters except the next play. Nothing. You have to be *emotionally selfish* before and during games, and you're the only one who can make sure you're in a Big Dog frame of mind.

Focus completely on your mental routines and physical skills. A little game watching isn't bad (at tournaments and when you're on the bench), but don't get emotionally involved. Save your energy for *your performance*. I'm not saying to not support your teammates, I am just suggesting saving your special emotional energy for yourself. Your team needs you to keep that special energy inside, so you can deliver the high-level play for everyone.

The less you engage what is going on around you the more focused you'll be on competing. Mentally control your competitive emotions, and everything else in life can wait until you're through competing for the day.

If you carefully use Battle Zone thinking, and follow your Confidence Routines precisely you will get to each play focused, confident, ready to compete.

Gear Issues

A key element to keeping your competitive mind focused is learning how to deal with the unexpected. Gear issues can be a little unnerving, even for a seasoned competitor. Leaving a piece of gear behind, losing it, or having a piece of gear break can be very distracting, so having a backup gear plan is not only smart, it's essential.

I've seen world-class competitors so emotionally attached to their gear that fellow competitors would purposefully steal or break their gear just to distract them and throw them off balance. It's actually funny to watch a world-class athlete fall apart because he doesn't have his "special" piece of gear.

So, what if a piece of gear breaks? First, don't react like a rookie; it's not that critical, so don't come unglued. Yes, it's your favorite, it feels the best, and you're the most comfortable with that particular piece of gear. So? It's gear. Shift gears (no pun intended) and make the necessary adjustments. Coaches will help you with the broken piece, deal with the distraction calmly, make the adjustments and compete.

No matter what goes wrong—because undoubtedly things will go wrong—remain composed. You're there to compete. Caring about gear is pure rookie distraction.

Practice During League Play

Practice narrowing your thinking to just the 4 Battle Zones and using your 7 Confidence Routines during league play leading up to districts, (sectionals), and state. The more familiar you are with narrowing your focus to the Battle Zones and using your Confidence Routines the more focused you'll be at the major "title" games, and the easier it will be to conquer the distractions of the stadium.

SUMMARY

- Block out stadium distractions.
- Narrow your thinking to the 4 Battle Zones to make every stadium familiar.
- Be able to turn laser beam focus on and off.
- Get horizontal (if possible) to rest and recover.
- Use your Confidence Routines many times each game to maintain emotional stability.
- Don't "act" serious, **be serious.**

"Recognizing the dangers of the stadium is one of the first steps towards learning how to compete. Whether at your high school field, an away game, or a big league stadium, game time distractions can be overwhelming. Narrow your thinking to manage the intensity and distractions of the stadium."

— Steve Knight

Chapter 3

NUTRITION • Game Fuel

Essential. Crucial. Vital. Critical. Do I have your attention? Nutrition is extremely important. Other than controlling doubt, I don't know of any other aspect of high-level competition that has greater importance.

One of the reasons nutrition doesn't get the attention it deserves: Most people haven't played all-out, do-or-die, game after game, day after day. They don't realize how draining high-level competition can be. But as you players know, at the end of a grueling game or demanding practice, there's nothing left in the gas tank.

Being able to have laser beam concentration, split second timing and instant reactions throughout an entire game and post season can make the

*"The best way to predict the future
is to create it."*

— Peter F. Drucker

difference between going home a champion or going home a loser. One missed clutch play because you were out of gas can end both your season and sometimes future opportunities. The importance of having quick, new energy for immediate recovery is essential.

Food Is Fuel

Think of food as more functional than emotional, especially for games; in other words, **detach your tongue**. Food is literally fuel. Don't just think about what tastes good, think about what your body and mind need to re-

Above: St. Peter's Tom Bistre (2) gets by the leg sweep of New Dorp's Ban Barbar. Photo by Hilton Flores/Staten Island Advance

Left: IU Men's Soccer celebrates a 3rd round victory over Boston College. Photo by Paul B. Riley/IU Athletics

cover and be ready for the next play. For outstanding game performance choose high-octane, quick recovery Big Dog fuel over weak, low-energy tongue food. You don't have to become a nutritionist in order to understand the basic differences between Big Dog fuel and tongue food. Stay with me here and I'll keep this as simple as possible.

Think of food in two groups: types and sources. Types: proteins, carbs, and fats. Sources: bad, good, and premium. Blending carbs and fats from premium sources results in high-octane, quick recovery Big Dog fuel.

Proteins

On game day, proteins are the least desirable type of food for one reason: the body doesn't use proteins as quick energy. The body uses proteins to rebuild muscle and other cells; it doesn't use protein as gasoline (energy). Before a game is not the time to rebuild cells. Before a game is the time to fill your gas tank.

Protein is a good thing at night, when you're through playing/ competing for the day. In fact, you ought to eat a little protein at end of the day for a variety of reasons.

The primary sources of protein are beef, poultry, and fish. A six-ounce can of tuna is perfect. Tuna is a great source of protein and other important nutrients (e.g. omega fats). Junk food: a processed burger, fries, and a shake or soda pop, have nothing, or very little that your body needs before a game or hard practice. And in fact, junk food is the last thing your body needs *after* an intense game or grueling practice. I'm not doggin' junk food, I'm criticizing poor, low-energy, mindless, tongue related choices. Do your best, at least during the season, and particularly before games, to eat from premium sources. You'll "feel" the difference. There will be more on premium sources later in this chapter.

Carbs & Fats

Carbs and fats are the types of food that provide immediately usable energy. Effectively combining carbs and fats is the key to having a *huge* gas tank.

Think of carbs and fats like the paper, twigs, and logs you would use to build a fire. The paper and twigs are carbs—quick fuel. Fats are the logs— denser, longer burning fuel. Proteins are like green wood that just lies there smoldering.

Split carbs into two categories: simple (paper) and complex (twigs). You want a little of each. Fruit is a simple carb (paper), and the quickest energy to get into the blood stream. The body doesn't have to do anything to fruit sugar in order to burn it.

Game Fuel
High-Octane Sources

Fast Burning Carbs:
Fruit - Apple (skinned)
Orange
Banana

Slow Burning Carbs:
Grain - Whole Wheat
Bread
Muffins
Bagels

Long Burning "Good" Fat:
Cream Cheese
String Cheese
Peanut Butter

Carb/Fat Combo:
Bagel & Cream Cheese
Bagel & Peanut Butter
Peanut Butter & Jelly
Nut Mix
Wrap or Sandwich

HYDRATION

70% Water   30% Sports Drinks

Posers eat, players fuel. On game day, be smart about food and fluids—*detach your tongue.*

Winning
STATE™
Soccer

Grains are complex carbs (twigs), which take your body a little longer to burn. The body has to work a little to digest grains, but they provide a longer burning energy stream, unlike fruit (paper), which is - poof, gone.

Fats are probably the least understood, but most important fuel for your competitive fire. Your body loves fat because it's concentrated, dense energy. There are twice as many calories (energy) in one gram of fat than there are in one gram of carbs. Fats are truly the logs for your body's furnace.

Some of the misinformation you may have read includes the notion that fat slows digestion. That's incorrect. The right way to look at fat is that it's **slower to digest.** Since fat has twice the energy, it burns slower, but that is a good thing.

"Don't just think of what tastes good, think of what your mind and body needs to recover, and be ready for the second half."

Example: Think of trying to start a blazing fire which will last for hours. If you use just paper and twigs, you can't do it. The fire will blaze for about 10 minutes and then die out. Not even a coal will be left. If you try and run on just carbs, you'll run out of fuel by the end of the game - when you need it most.

Again, the key to building a great fire—having a huge gas tank—is combining carbs and fats, which is short-term energy and long-term energy.

Review the high-octane Game Fuel examples, and limit yourself to those choices. At least during the season and especially before games, think with your Big Dog mindset, not with your tongue. Manage your food choices for championship level outstanding performances.

Premium Sources

Premium sources of game fuel and fluids come from nature. They haven't been processed or modified from their original state. This is a pretty simple concept to understand. If food has gone through a machine; had anything taken from it or added to it; it's been processed. Processed food is

Fuel Sequence
Water + Carbs + Fats

Water + Fruit + Combo + Combo

REAL FOOD is optimum; stay away from processed junk.
Combine carbs and fats for superior energy levels.

Below: Protein options for road trips, and after games/practices:

| Grilled Fish/Chicken Pasta/Rice/Veggies | Stuffed Potato | Turkey Sandwich | Chicken Wrap |

Combine carbs and fats to maintain high-energy levels on game day. *Be smart about nutrition—fuel, don't eat.*

Winning
STATE™
Soccer

tongue food, not body and mind food. Nature provides premium game fuel, not machines.

Man-made *products*, like protein bars, the majority of the time have been altered, preservatives have been added for longer shelf life and flavor enhancers have been added to make them good tongue food. This processing alters the structure of the food and makes it harder for your body to burn efficiently. The additives are an additional issue, but I won't go into how unhealthy processed foods are, I'll just stay focused on their burning capability.

A little real-time clarification is in order. It's the winter of 2005 and healthy snacks are on the rise. Some "bar" companies are making their products with organic, pure ingredients. If you like the convenience of bars, do a little research and look at the ingredients list. Choose a brand which uses only natural ingredients (oats, fruit, peanut butter, etc.) If you can't pronounce an ingredient, typically it's not real. Get the picture? If you have to buy a packaged product, buy one that is both good for you and a great source of fuel.

The other problem with most bars is that they're very low in calories, and extremely low in fat. Typically most bars are around 200-230 calories with under 5 grams of fat. For most of you, that means about 20 minutes worth of medium grade fuel, even if you choose a bar from premium sources. So, if you eat a bar at half time thinking you're completely fueling up, you're not; within 20 minutes of the second half you'll be out of gas. A bagel and cream cheese, a Peanut Butter & Jelly San, or a nut mix are much better than a bar. You need ample fuel, not taste.

Back to non-premium sources: burgers, fries, and shakes, plus plastic cheese, chips, and hot dogs from the concession stand, are not premium game fuel sources. I hope this information is getting inside that tongue driven head, and you're starting to see the difference between Little Dog tongue food, and Big Dog game fuel.

You can eat poisonous junk (processed food) all year long if you need to - Yuck! But I encourage you to consume mostly high-octane Big Dog game fuel during the season. Look past your tongue and think about what your mind and body need to recover from the extreme energy drain of long practices and intense games.

Review the diagram of Game Fuel sources and stick as close to that as possible for optimum results. The key thing to remember—**food is fuel**—*detach your tongue.*

Game Meal

The first type of food to consume a couple of hours before a game should be a real piece of fruit: banana, orange, or apple. You know the reason, right? Consume a simple carb (paper) first, which will immediately put

Above: Mililani's Ehren Ching, left, shields the ball from Kalaheo's Dominic Simon in the first half of the OIA boys soccer championship. Photo by Eugene Tanner/The Honolulu Advertiser

fuel in your tank. It will quickly increase your blood sugar level, and you'll feel fueled instantly.

After the initial piece of fruit, and water, comes a carb/fat combo: a bagel and cream cheese, bagel and peanut butter, or PB&J, plus a nut mix on the side. Stay away from meat.

The amount of carb/fat combo you need depends on your size. If you're less than 150 pounds you may only need one bagel, but if you're 175 pounds plus, you may need a couple of them.

The key thing to keep in mind—don't overdo it. Control yourself. Don't make yourself uncomfortable. Take a break and let your digestive system break down the food. After 20 minutes or so, if you're still not full, go back for more, but during the second round you can *skip the fruit*. Go for another carb/fat combo. After you've reached the full line, it's time to take a break. There's probably at least one hour before starting pre-game warm-ups, so put on your headphones, calm your mind, GET HORIZONTAL (if possible), and let your body absorb the mass quantities, while you prepare your mind for battle with Big Dog Visualization.

Half Time

I rarely see teams provide fuel in the locker room during half time, which is a bit of a mystery to me. If I were running the show, there would be ample quantities of premium fuel before the game and during half time: fresh fruit, bagels and cream cheese, PB&J sandwiches, nut mixes, and gallons of water.

"Burgers, fries, and a shake are not optimum fuel sources. The plastic cheese, chips, and hot dogs at the concession stand aren't either."

If your team is not one that provides fuel, put it on your list of Big Dog necessities and bring it with you. It's not that tough; throw a couple of items in your backpack and watch your teammates beg for scraps.

Colored Sugar Water

This is such an ugly subject. You guys hate this information.

Despite what the companies who sell it want you to think, like it or not, colored sugar water isn't all that. The claim of "optimally replenishing vital electrolytes and nutrients" is a marketing ploy to sell more drinks.

Our bodies are 70 percent WATER, not 70 percent sports drink. So when you've sweat a couple pounds of water, you need to replenish it with water.

There is so much garbage in many of the "ade" drinks: dyes, sugars, preservatives, etc., that your body has to work at discarding the garbage in order to use the water left behind.

The refined sugar in those "ade" drinks is not good fuel; so don't buy into the claim that they will help you replenish spent energy faster. Real, unprocessed fruit sugar (already explained) will get in your blood stream faster, and burn better. Don't confuse a piece of fruit with drinking gallons of fruit juice. A large amount of fruit juice is not recommended because it's

Above: Gateway's Goalie Andy Rida and Hopkin's Jon Chan tumble over in an attempt to control the ball, just feet away from the goal. Photo by Mieke Zuiderweg

too acidic and will cause digestive issues. To be very clear, I'm not advocating *hydrating* with fruit juice. I'm suggesting eating a single piece of fruit before a game and during half time in order to elevate your blood sugar - *hydrate with water.*

Sports drink salesman love to talk about electrolytes. But more sodium is not the cure for getting your electrolytes back in balance either. In fact, over salting (salt tablets) can cause problems. A simple multi-mineral tablet will do more for replenishing electrolytes, and will also help you keep from cramping.

Just "Google" "replenish electrolytes" and you'll see what I'm talking about. Look for sources that aren't selling anything, and you'll get the straight information.

If you have to use sports drinks because of tongue preference, use them sparingly in combination with water, like a 70/30 mix. That means 70 percent water. I'm not talking about mixing them together—seven glasses of water to three glasses of sports drink. However, after playing in the extreme heat and you've sweat off pounds of fluids you should stick with water until you get your fluid level back up where it needs to be. Then include some sports drink if you can't control your tongue.

One of the real dangers of colored sugar water, the "ade" drinks, is you become tongue addicted, and won't drink water, so you fail to hydrate as much as you need to.

Example: If you're a big sweater on a blistering hot day in the 90's, by the end of practice or a game you're totally dehydrated. Why? Do the math: It's easy to sweat off several (6-10) pounds of water in the extreme heat. This makes hydrating with colored sugar-water difficult; it's too syrupy (sugar) and has too much junk in it. Instinctively, you'll stop hydrating after a couple of pounds of sports drink. Get the mental picture? A monster sports drink container, the big one, is 64 ounces (4 pounds). You would need to drink at least two during the course of a game for proper hydration. You won't do it, so you get dehydrated, and by the end of the game you'll be confused and disoriented.

Simply put, hydration is about function, not taste. Remove taste from the equation. In other words—Little Dogs focus on taste, Big Dogs focus on fuel. So, Little Dogs, get over it.

"Little dogs focus on taste, while Big Dogs focus on fuel."

Above: Tottenville's Andrea DiGregorio (32) and McKee Staten Island Tech's Teddy Cesar chase down a loose ball. Photo by Hilton Flores/SI Advance

Don't Change A Thing

This may be confusing. I've told you to focus on fuel, not junk. Now I'm telling you: "don't change a thing." What I mean is, if you don't add some high-octane fuel to your diet, in order to let your body get used to digesting good food, it might not be a good idea to make drastic changes on game day

Sometimes a junk digestive system has a hard time with dense energy foods. If you're a Pop-Tart, sugared cereal breakfast eater, a bagel and cream cheese might cause some digestive problems the first couple of times. Before games you want to stay as close to your "standard" food routine as possible; it's what your body knows.

During Tournaments: Nutrition is significant. And if nutrition (fueling) isn't a key factor in your tournament preparation—get it there! Whether it's the pre-season or post-season, tournaments make it hard for your body and mind to recover. In a tournament situation, time is against you. You don't get days to rest between games; you get hours. Therefore, if you want to win, every choice, every bite is critical! Premium fuel is the key. Without high-octane quick recovery fuel you won't consistently shoot well, pass well, or defend well—simple as that. Good nutrition and hydration are also important for solid sleep. Ever try to sleep on a stomach full of pizza and sugar-drinks? Being able to sprint continuously, run the field from end to end, and still have legs in the final minutes is also about good sleep. If you don't fuel right, you won't sleep right—and then you won't have the gas tank to compete at your highest level. Competing is about focusing men-tally, and your mind can't do it if your body is screaming for good fuel, hydration, and rest.

For outstanding performances during season, add some high-octane game fuel to your daily and weekly food intake. This does two things: it familiarizes your body with dense energy foods, and it helps you recover and rebuild more quickly during the week.

Another example of "don't change a thing" ties to your first meal of the day when you're out-of-town at away games, especially big title games. Be careful about going to a restaurant for the "great" breakfast before the "big" day. Emotionally that sounds and feels good, but unless you've eaten the

Above: Moore Catholic goalie Ray Beshara, left, and Port Richmond's Luca Giacona. Photo by Hilton Flores/Staten Island Advance

"great" breakfast at that restaurant before, it's not a good idea. Remember, stay with what your body knows. Eating breakfast at an unfamiliar restaurant on game day is *high risk*. You don't know what you're going to get. Plus, just because you're in the playoffs doesn't mean it's time to celebrate.

If going to a restaurant is a must, you want to be smart about your choices. Bacon and eggs, hash browns, toast, pancakes, biscuits and gravy; are all tongue and taste habit related choices. Get rid of the bacon; add some fat (real butter) to the pancakes, and who knows about the biscuits and gravy. Personally, the morning of a big game I wouldn't even consider going to an unfamiliar restaurant. *Not a chance!*

Remember: Game day is not the day to indulge your taste buds. Save that for after the game, a victory dinner is all-good.

S U M M A R Y

- Think of food as fuel.

- Forget taste. Go for types of food your mind and body need to recover.

- Grab fruit for an instant boost.

- Combine good carbs and fats to sustain maximum energy levels.

- Save proteins for after the game to rebuild muscle and other cells.

- Hydrate primarily with water.

- **Detach your tongue.** Fuel, don't eat.

"The information and recommendations in this chapter have special meaning, which extend beyond elevating your game performance. Choosing what type of food to consume daily: Organic vs. processed, is one of life's critical decisions.

Look around, ask questions, understand that food is more important than what we like or dislike. Do yourself good; get interested in understanding the difference between processed tongue food and organic healthy food."   — Steve Knight

Chapter 4

ATTITUDE • Game Mode

As competitors, we live or die by attitude.

In the introduction, I mentioned how I've watched numerous stud players lose before the game even starts. Actually, I've witnessed countless athletes from a wide variety of sports, on all levels, deal with the same problem. Doubt demons dominate their thinking centers, and they mentally submit long before the physical competition ever begins. They haven't learned how to control their emotions during competition.

When athletes experience severe doubt, which I call "a meltdown," they have a certain look—almost like going into shock. Their eyes glaze over, they don't respond well to conversation and they become distant. Mentally they choke, because they haven't learned how to believe in themselves under pressure.

"Attitude is everything!"

— Jeff Jordan

**Above: A poster titled "Death's End" from artist Ken Kelly.
See more of Ken Kelly's warrior art at www.kenkellyart.com.
Left: NCAA Championships IU vs. UCSB. Players unknown.
Photo by Paul B. Riley/IU Athletics**

Don't Deny It

Over the years I've worked with hundreds of athletes from a variety of sports on how to manage doubt and fear in competition. The bottom line is, we don't get anywhere as competitors unless we openly realize that doubt and fear are inevitable. When we truly hunger to win, but still recognize the possibility of losing or not performing to our full potential, doubt and fear are the natural result. For some, the nervous emotion associated with pressure situations, not knowing the outcome of a competition, can be paralyzing; for others, the unknown is exciting. Even the most experienced world-class competitor has moments of doubt, fear, and intimidation; it's natural. Learning how to perform well under pressure is about dealing with doubt. When we don't hide from the truth, we can look our doubt demons square in the face and deal with them. But when we deny doubt by not being truthful with ourselves, our doubt demons grab us by the throat, which is like committing competitive suicide, because we're doing it to ourselves. The key to superior performance under pressure is learning how to openly detect and then control doubt, fear, and intimidation.

"Doubt and fear are a reality a competitor has to live with his entire career; it's just the way it is."

For those of you who are thinking, "I never get scared," that's OK; you're either in denial or winning is not that important to you. But for those of us who really want to win, when we're up against a strong, worthy opponent and our minds are battling the possibility of failure, we get scared. Doubt and fear are a reality a competitor has to live with his entire career. Doubt and fear are part of being a competitive athlete; it's just the way it is.

Puppies

Before we get into the process of developing a Game Mode perspective, let's go back to the beginning—when we were all puppies.

Realize this: even the most dominant competitor was a little puppy at some point. Why is this an important point? Because we all start out at the same place—as helpless infants—*all of us.*

Then, when we begin to grow and our genetics take over; some puppies naturally bite, and some puppies don't. The real question is: *Can passive puppies learn to be aggressive dogs?* Answer: Yes they can.

A wolf pack is a good way to illustrate this point. In a pack of 10, there are a couple of Big Dogs who constantly duke-it-out for the top position. The middle dogs fight for positions three through seven and the Little Dogs are reduced to the bottom positions in the pack, fighting for the scraps. Those social positions are decided when wolves are puppies, and rarely do those positions change as adults.

A wolf's position within the pack is determined by its genetics, its inherent size and testosterone level:

Physically Large/aggressive: Big Dog
Physically Medium/assertive: Mid Dog
Physically Small/submissive: Little Dog

However, unlike wolves, we humans are very different; it is sooooo important for you middle and Little Dogs to realize this: unlike wolves, we can recognize our "natural" tendencies, and through careful planning and training we can elevate our basic born-to genetics.

Above: Some puppies bite and some puppies don't. Can passive puppies learn how to be aggressive dogs?

Pay attention here! This is one of the key concepts I'm trying to express in this book: for human beings, where we fit on the Dog Scale—little to big —is *up to us.*

Those of us who are more naturally the alpha male—the Big Dog— probably have a competitive advantage, but only while we're puppies. Once Little Dogs figure out that being a Big Dog is mostly about attitude, a transformation takes place. Little dogs can learn how to show some teeth and let their Big Dog out!

Guys, we never earn respect just by winning. We earn respect by fighting, by constantly battling for position, by giving it everything we've got and never mentally giving up. *It's not about the size of the dog in the fight; it's about the size of the fight in the dog.* Will and guts define the size of the fight: executing with genuine confidence in pressure situations. Determination and guts have nothing to do with physical size or strength. *Guts come from attitude.*

No matter where our genetics initially put us on the Dog Scale, whether little or big, to be a winner we must become more than just our natural genetics. Stay with me here. Big Dogs go over the top, while Little Dogs don't show up. Big Dogs underestimate their opponents, while Little Dogs overestimate their opponents. Big Dogs are shocked when they lose, while Little Dogs are shocked when they win. Both Big and Little Dogs have detrimental characteristics that require wise, assertive control.

If I had to bet on either a Little Dog who has learned to let his Big Dog out versus a kid who has been a Big Dog all his life, I'll take the Little Dog any day. The Little Dog has more to prove, its need is deeper and fiercer. Most of the time an "underdog" is just a Little Dog with an attitude, someone who will bleed to the end rather than give up. That's how we earn re-

Above: A great shot of the wolf pack. Socially, where do you fit? Little dog or Big Dog? Be real with yourself. It's the firs step towards controlling your competitive minds. Photographer unknown.

Above: Like humans, wolves have many sides to their personalities. Being able to switch from affection to fierce dominance—in an instant— is a skill a competitor has to have. Photographer unknown.

spect. Face the opponent and be ready to take an arrow in the forehead, but never take one in the back. You all know what this is about. When a good forward takes the pass in the win-zone he doesn't think about the defenders in front of him—all he sees is the net.

I hope you Little Dogs get this point. The only reason you're a Little Dog is because you think you're a Little Dog. All of us, every single one of us, has a Big Dog deep inside; we just have to find him and learn how to let him out! When Little Dogs realize their Big Dog is waiting to play, and they just have to let him out, everything changes.

Welcome It

The first step to developing your Game Mode perspective is recognizing when you're going into a doubt meltdown—don't fight it. Welcome the butterflies and the doubt. Step back, breathe, and resurrect those positive Big Dog images of previous successful performances. Get yourself back to that centered, confident, frame of mind—a serious Game Mode mindset.

Personal story: In 1983, I was competing in the US Senior National Powerlifting Championships, which at the time was the most competitive tournament of the year, more so than even the world championships.

"The first step to developing your Game Mode perspective is recognizing when you're going into a meltdown—don't fight it."

I was in the best shape of my career, and lifted in the 181-pound weight class. In a Powerlifting competition, the squat is the first lift. I was going to attempt a personal record, which at the time was only a few pounds off a world record. You get three attempts; the first two are basically warm-ups. My first attempt at 644 pounds was easy. My second at 683 pounds was incredibly solid—I felt great. I picked 722 pounds for my third and final attempt. It was my turn, and in Powerlifting when your name is called you have three minutes to get the weight out of the squat rack or you're disqualified.

Nationals were being held in a huge arena with a few thousand people attending. As I walked on and took control of the platform I was in a great mental place. I was totally confident, or so I thought.

As I reached for and took hold of the bar, a little voice from demon land said, "Your going to fail," and instantly I got this mental picture of taking the weight out of the rack, my legs breaking off at the knees, and the weight driving me straight down through the platform.

This obviously broke my concentration. I looked up and actually laughed out loud. It startled me and it came from nowhere. I backed away from the weight, took a couple of deep breaths, told the little demon voice

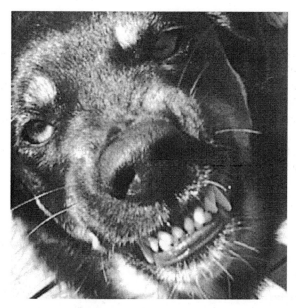

Above: The real deal. Photo source: Whole-Dog-Journal.com.

where to go, and brought back the feelings of my solid warm-ups, memories of successful "big" lifts in the past, and approached the bar for a second time. Doubt resurfaced slightly, but mentally I was full of confidence and plowed ahead.

I made the lift, and in doing so set an Oregon state record that still stands today.

What's the moral of the story? Doubt and fear will surface at the worst possible moment. Being able to control doubt under pressure is what makes an athlete clutch. Program your mind to be able to maintain composure by looking doubt square in the face, conquering it and executing.

Detect It

First, I must acknowledge that a soccer player's doubt intensity is unique. The variables are extreme. Big stadiums, complex game situations, and "team" emotions are different than, for example: a weightlifter or an ice skater. I'm not taking anything away from those other athletes, especially since I was one of them; I'm just being real.

Think about it. As a weightlifter I always knew who my opponent was—no confusion, no gray area. 700 pounds is 700 pounds whether it's in New York, Los Angeles or Tokyo. 700 pounds can't convince itself to be 900 pounds.

An ice skater has a similar situation. Yeah, the ice is different from arena to arena, but the difference is not that significant. The ice isn't going to jump up and slam the skater down. The weightlifter and ice skater's doubt demons are very different than a soccer player's.

A soccer player's doubt and intimidation are magnified significantly because he looks a live competitor directly in the eyes. A soccer player's opponent is truly unknown, and *it's alive*. Even if a player has been up against a particular opponent many times before, it's still an unknown. A soccer player has to *master* doubt and fear or his opponent will run right through him.

Above: Alexander's soccer team. Player unknown. Photo by Stefan Bruckel

Doubt Meter
BIG-DOG Detector

10.0 RED ALERT, major meltdown, Little Dogs just wet the turf — all confidence gone.

7.5 Extreme panic, partial meltdown, crumbling.

5.0 Threshold of losing it.

4.0 Genuine doubt, panic.
3.5 Tweaked, but manageable.
3.0 Slightly tweaked.

2.0 Uncertain—composed—Big Dog.

1.0 Butterflies—composed—Big Dog.

0.0 Calm—composed—Big Dog.

Doubt is inevitable. Denying it is fatal. Learn to detect Little Dog doubt before you crash and burn.

When you're intimidated and your confidence is crashing, be truthful; don't pretend it's not. Use **Big Dog Visualization** to regain your composure.

"It's not the size of the dog in the fight, it's the size of the fight in the dog."

— Dwight D. Eisenhower

All of you who have competed in intense game situations know that you have your hands full with your own emotions and the natural ups and downs of insecurity and self-doubt. So programming your mind and doing everything possible to put yourself in the right place emotionally is what will help you deliver consistent, superior play.

Back to the process.

The first step in managing doubt and fear is learning how to detect a meltdown before reaching the critical point, which is easy to do if we're truthful with ourselves.

When we feel dominant, doubt and fear are not an issue. It's when we feel inferior or uncertain that doubt and fear become major factors in our ability to perform. And it's completely natural. When something triggers feelings of insecurity, our two competitive minds, "I can't vs. I can," go into the confidence battle. We flip-flop back and forth from confident to doubtful, especially when the pressure is on and we really want to succeed. But keep in mind that pressure is not the doubt trigger; it's something else.

Above: A Washington player grabs a handful of Seyi Abolaji's jersey during a Stanford win. Photo by David Gonzales

Left: Douey Wright (center). Photo source City College of New York

In a pressure situation, if we're up against an opposing player that we know we can beat, we're licking our chops for the opportunity to shine. That little voice in our head is saying, "Bring it on." Doubt triggers are usually intimidation based, and when pressure is added, BAM! We go into a meltdown.

Detecting doubt is as simple as identifying any other emotion. We know when we're happy, sad or angry. Doubt is no different. The problem is, when it comes to doubt, we often hide from the truth. The first step, as expressed previously, is to not deny it. Be truthful and say to yourself, "I'm nervous." Laugh it off, sort of a "duh" moment, and talk yourself down.

Talk Yourself Down

When doubt and fear have you by the throat it's like committing competitive suicide; you're doing it to yourself—you're a "jumper." Once you can be truthful with yourself and comfortably detect a meltdown, the next step is being able to recover by talking yourself down. The process is simple to understand, but hard to do.

To calm ourselves down we must take our minds to a different place. Whatever we were focusing on that made us feel inferior; we need to disconnect that line of thinking. As I've said before, meltdown triggers are things like: that forward has incredibly quick feet, that midfielder is a hard tackler, or that team is undefeated.

The trick to disconnecting the intimidating line of negative thinking is to force your mind to think about actual, real experiences when *you* were "clutch." It doesn't matter when; they just need to be real experiences you can "believe" in. The key is to make your mind go where you want it to, because fear is all in your mind. As I've tried to express several times, the battle that will makes you a champion is fought in your mind, not on the field. *And those who believe win.* A great president once said, "The only thing we have to fear is fear itself."

This process of welcoming, detecting, and controlling doubt is presented in greater detail in Chapter 5. You're going to learn Big Dog Visualization, which is much more than positive thinking; it is "replacement" thinking. You're going to learn how to replace negative visions (fantasies) of failure with actual experiences when you were successful.

Personal story: A couple of years ago when my youngest son was wrestling in high school I traveled with his team to the Reno Tournament of Champions. Most of you soccer players won't be familiar with that tournament, but Reno is one of the most prestigious national wrestling tournaments of the season. The level of talent is seriously deep in every weight class. It would be like the top soccer teams from across the country traveling to a specific town for a 10 game championship over three days. Keep in mind that the techniques I'm teaching are for all sports; actually they're for all of life's pressure situations, so in the following story pay attention to the emotional roller coaster this athlete went through, not the wrestling details. My son's team had a couple of wrestlers who, if they showed up emotionally, had the potential to place or win.

I was sort of the team mom. I shuttled the team back and forth from the hotel, kept the tournament fuel flowing, and helped the coaches and athletes with whatever they needed. Many of the wrestlers from the team were rookies at a tournament of that size—they didn't win a match. But, a couple of our guys made it to the medal rounds.

One of our middleweights—152 lbs—whom I'll call "Our Guy" was wrestling for third/fourth, and at this tournament the top 3 placers received All-American status—it was a big deal.

I was chilling in the stands watching the competition as the lighter weight classes started. Our Guy came up and asked if I'd seen the coaches. He didn't look good—sort of clammy and grayish. I thought to myself, "Oh man, he's going into a meltdown." I told him I didn't know where the coaches were and he took off.

A couple of minutes later he came back and was having problems with a kneepad. The kneepad really wasn't a problem of any significance, but

Game Mode
A Serious Mindset

Game Mode is a serious mindset; it's about steely eyed, piercing concentration—NO acting, NO pretending, NO faking. It's about precision laser beam concentration on a specific target.

Narrow your focus; block out distractions; stabilize your competitive confidence; Game Mode is about winning, not playing.

Get serious. Learn to focus and believe.

Above: Game face. Photo source: neptunesoccer.com

**"You have to expect things of yourself
before you can do them."**

— Michael Jordan

when you're in a meltdown *everything* is catastrophic. In the middle of telling me about the kneepad, he turned and took off. He was coming unglued.

I went and found the coaches on the arena floor and told them that Our Guy was coming apart. They really didn't know what to do. "What does he need," they asked?

I told them he was talking about a kneepad problem, but actually he was just getting emotionally tweaked about his match. Even though these coaches had numerous first-hand experiences with "tweaked" athletes, they really didn't know how to recognize a meltdown, nor did they have the experience in talking someone down and then back up to competitive confidence.

Warm-ups: We've all gone through pre-game warm-ups. Each time we head out on that field, we see our opponents down at the other end, and it's normal to size them up. Do they look skilled? Have you seen them on film? Are they a real physical team? Great speed? Quick to the ball? However, from a confidence standpoint none of those assessments matter. Focusing on their abilities will only cause you to question your own, or worse, send you into a meltdown. If you overestimate our opponents, doubt is almost certain to appear. If it does, don't ignore it—that's a Little Dog tendency, which leads to self-destruction. Welcome the butterflies and detect the meltdown before it happens. Remember: doubt is inevitable, denying it is fatal. Learn how to visualize yourself back to confidence.

Right about then Our Guy found us on the arena floor. He told the coaches about his kneepad issues, and one coach went off to find him another kneepad. One of the other coaches said, "You'll be fine," slapped him on the shoulder and that was supposedly going to be the end of it. But I could tell this kid was ready to throw up.

Respectfully, I told the head coach (who is an awesome man) that Our Guy needed to be talked down and asked if I could work with him. I got the green light, and asked Our Guy to go for a walk. I put my arm around his shoulder, and as we walked to the other end of the arena, I asked him, "Do you like homework?" He looked at me and could barely get the answer out, "No, not really." "Got a girl friend?" "Yeah." "You like to go fishing?"

"What?" he asked. "What about cars? You like cars?" I just started asking random questions. He got really confused, but as we talked about absolutely nothing, reality started creeping back in. The random real world questions were disengaging his fear. It's fascinating to watch someone's mind come back from extreme lost-in-fear mode.

Once I started to see his eyes clear and his mind calm down, I asked him why his opponent was in his kitchen. He sparked a little grin. "Because he beat me yesterday in the semi's." With that statement, Our Guy saw his fear and was able to be *real* with himself. Keep in mind that whoever won the upcoming match would receive All American status. Placing at Reno was a BIG deal nationally. You got ink in national papers and magazines, and as a high schooler that only helps ones college prospects.

"So basically you can't win," I said. "No, I *can* win," he snapped right back. "How?" I asked with a *whatever* kind of a tone. Our Guy started listing his opponent's strengths and weaknesses; he relived the match from the day before out loud. By the end of his description he was amused at why he was so tweaked. "I can beat this kid," he said with some conviction. I laughed, shoved him, and said, "Exactly." We went back over those real time positive thoughts and mental images several times. I told Our Guy to keep his mind right where it was: On his strengths and his opponent's weaknesses.

A few minutes later Our Guy was back on Earth. His competitive confidence was solid and he was looking forward to kicking some butt. He laid around chilling until it was time to get into his pre-match warm-ups. He was in a great place mentally and had a totally different look and feel.

Our Guy dominated the match and pinned his archrival in the third period. It was an exciting match to watch. Our Guy is an All American.

The story continues.

Those two wrestled each other again at other tournaments twice before state. Our Guy beat his rival soundly both times. Our Guy owned him, or so it seemed.

At state Our Guy was ranked No. 1 and his rival was ranked No. 2. The rankings played out, and they were in the finals. This was going to be an awesome match; we all fully expected, of course, that Our Guy would emerge state champion.

I was not in the trenches with the team at state, so I watched from the stands. As the match began, I could see within seconds that Our Guy was tweaked. He opened tentatively and was soon on his heels. Our Guy's rival was also tentative. He had been beaten three times in the previous two months. However, once he realized that Our Guy was uncertain, he gained a huge confidence advantage and turned it on. If you know what you're looking for you can see it as you watch the match on video.

In the second period Our Guy rolled his ankle. He did his best to recover, but couldn't. His rival hung on and defended well in the third period to become state champion. What a year.

Our Guy owned his opponent during the season. He had beaten his rival three times previously under tremendous pressure, but his doubt let his rival back in the game during the state tournament. The worst part was that all that doubt was pure fantasy.

All of you have seen or lived a story like this and it is so important to realize—it's all in your mind.

Composure

Once you've learned how to welcome and detect doubt and fear and then how to talk yourself down, you'll gain a tremendous amount of confidence in the process, because your mind and emotions will be focused on your strengths and actual experiences when you succeeded. The more skilled you become at this process of detection and control, the easier it will be to stay confident. The dramatic flip-flopping from confident to doubtful will be less intense and less frequent, because you'll be ready for doubt and fear to creep up when your opponent is formidable or there is a title on the

Above: Hillsborough soccer. Players unknown. Photo source pbase.com

line. You'll recognize doubt triggers and be looking for them; but rather than going into a meltdown you'll be mentally equipped to control and channel it.

Overtime: You've played a hard game all the way through, but it isn't over yet. In overtime you have to know how the game has gone, and what adjustments you want to make. Maybe your team fought to come from behind, maybe you fought hard and but haven't played your best, or maybe your team lost the lead. As overtime begins, mentally put behind you any negative thoughts from the game. Sure, you probably missed some plays, had shots blocked, or maybe your defense broke down a time or two, but as you head into OT none of that matters. Breathe, compose yourself, focus on your skills, and mentally replay all of your success from the game—go forward, and compete.

Competing successfully is about composure. When we're composed, we're not lost in that inner land of self-doubt. When we're confident and involved with the external, outer environment, we automatically see the cracks in our opponent's armor, which is what we need to do if we're going to leave the battlefield with our head still connected to our neck.

I encourage you to read the "Interviews Section" in the last part of the book. Pay close attention to each of the champion's descriptions of the importance of confidence for high-level play, and how they overcame doubt under pressure and succeeded. It's quite interesting. Almost every story is when they were not supposed to win, when they were in the championship game for the big title and they pulled it off by *believing* in themselves. I didn't ask these champions to describe a game when they were an underdog. I just asked them to describe a situation when they were doubtful, but kept it together and won.

Of course it makes sense; the time they rose to the occasion, conquered their fears, and made the big play are the times they're most proud of. And they should be. That's what competing is all about: *Maintaining confidence and composure under extreme pressure and executing.*

It's a tremendous personal accomplishment when we can maintain composure under pressure. Most of the time we're not as outmatched as we think we are. Most of the time our opponent isn't as good as we think he is. Yes, sometimes we do find ourselves up against someone who is going to blow by us no matter how well we execute. They just have more experience or greater physical prowess. But the majority of the time we give our opponents way more credit than they deserve.

So what do you do when you're up against someone who has the edge? Stay composed and learn something. If you go into battle as a mental midget you won't learn a thing. You accept defeat, which reinforces a Little Dog mentality. Not good. This is when you can practice controlling your mind by controlling and channeling your doubts and fears. This is something that always amazes me about athletes; if you're truly outmatched, why get shook up? Why not go out there and surprise both your opponent and yourself? Go show your opponent you're a competitor. You have nothing to lose and everything to gain.

Game Mode

Now the transformation begins. Once you learn how to detect and control your emotions you can transform from a mere player into a championship competitor—a warrior; it truly is a transformation, and the transformation is completely based on *believing in yourself.*

A true warrior doesn't care if his adversary is 10′ tall and weights 500 pounds. A true warrior is going to suck it up and execute. It's like breaking boards in martial arts. A beginning student can't even break one board. Then, in a short time, he can break three, then five, then seven. What happens? The student not only learns better physical techniques, like using his hips and striking the board squarely, but more importantly the student learns how to believe and penetrate—to strike *through* the board.

Those lessons totally apply to soccer players. Effective play is about penetration—to confidently out position your opponent and to put the ball were you want to put it. It's not about trying, it's about doing. If we're not confident and we don't believe, you'll get crushed, and end up short. It's a cause and effect relationship. If the guy who is trying to break five boards hesitates, he's going to break his knuckles. A warrior doesn't try to defeat the dragon; he slays it. No matter what, a warrior has *unflinching confidence that obliterates doubt and destroys hesitation.*

Game Mode is about being serious; it's about attitude. It's about leaving your real life in the parking lot and stepping into a competitive frame of mind. It's about developing the mental perspective that transforms passive puppies into aggressive dogs. It's about developing a second set of skills: The mental skills of a competitor. Game Mode is about stepping-up with confidence, and competing—to win.

S U M M A R Y

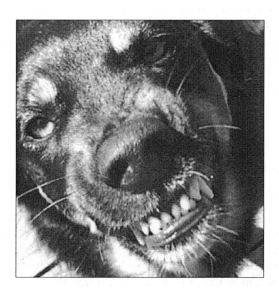

- Change your position on the Dog Scale.

- Don't hide from the truth.

- Welcome doubt and fear.

- Use the Doubt Meter to detect a meltdown.

- Talk yourself down, don't be a jumper.

- Compose yourself with Big Dog Visualization.

- Executing under pressure takes guts. Guts are about attitude.

"Remember: Doubt is inevitable, but choking is preventable. When we truthfully look at how we react emotionally in competition, and then master the techniques for controlling our Dogs, we're able to step-up and compete, with confidence." — Steve Knight

Chapter 5

Big Dog Visualization

If there's one chapter I encourage you to read over and over until you understand and master what is presented, it is this one.

Get real, learn to visualize, and believe. Controlling your mind and emotions is the battle that will make you a champion.

As I watch athletes train and prepare for state and national level competitions, there's one thing that perplexes me: Even after repeated failure most athletes have not realized that harnessing their emotions is just as or even more important than developing their physical skills and improving conditioning.

"Courage is not the absence of fear, but the ability to carry on in spite of it."

— Mark Twain

Above: Hueneme High School's Ricardo Martinez, right, races down the field as Oxnard's mid-fielder Bryan Zubiate attempts a steal. Photo by Jon Austria

Left: Newark Academy's Theodore Aronson has the ball headed over him by Montclair-Kimberly's Joe Walter (17). Photo by Jim Wright/Star-Ledger

Think of it this way: Why labor over technique and grind through conditioning if you don't believe in yourself? Why practice your brains out if you can't control the intense emotions that come with state and national level competition?

Personally, the reason I competed was to win the title tournaments. In order to accomplish that, my emotions had to be my friends—not my enemy.

Unique Approach

Typically, visualization is thought of as seeing victory – imagining yourself blazing by a defender and scoring the winning goal as the crowd erupts. Another common technique to offset doubt and intimidation is positive self-talk—mentally repeating positive statements attempting to convince yourself you're not really scared. I never had much success with either of those methods, because they didn't get at the root of the issue: **No matter how experienced we are, in pressure situations we're going to get scared, and negative emotions have to be managed.**

With help from my first coach, and through a lot of trial and error over years of competing, I developed what I call Big Dog Visualization—a unique approach to visualization. Instead of visualizing victory or repeating positive statements, Big Dog Visualization is about *replacing* doubt and intimidation with previous experiences when you where genuinely confident, and made big plays. In other words, you run over and over in your head all of the times you were successful; real experiences when you were clutch. Not fantasies, or mental projections of what you want to do, but actual, genuine, game-time memories when you delivered under pressure. Why? Because your mind and your heart can believe in what you have done—sort of the 'been there, done that' mindset. Stay with me here, and by the end of this chapter you'll know how to replace negative doubt and intimidation with positive success and accomplishment.

Two Minds

As I explained in the previous chapter, we all have two minds – our Little Dog mind and our Big Dog mind. Both minds have different sets of detrimental emotions, which have to be understood and managed in order to be successful in pressure situations. Our Little Dog mind is full of doubt and never thinks it can accomplish anything; it dwells on the negative. On the other hand, our Big Dog mind is sometimes overly confident and often focuses on the wrong things. To be a successful competitor (not just a soccer player, but a confident, clutch competitor) it's necessary to understand both of your minds, so you can effectively manage your emotions in pressure situations.

Rough Territory

Big Dog Visualization puts us in touch with our competitive minds— both of them. For many of us this is rough territory. Looking truthfully at ourselves is not something very many of us want to do.

But, if we want to be successful competitors, not just athletes, we have no choice. To command control over our emotions, we have to know where they come from. That's why envisioning victory or chanting positive statements is not very effective. Those techniques don't help us deal with the core issue: doubt will always be part of competing. Ignoring those emotions or trying to talk them away is an illusion and won't help the process of building true, reliable, high-level competitive confidence.

Learning how to see and feel your Big Dog isn't hard, if you're willing to look beyond the image you project and be truthful with yourself.

Get Real
Look At Yourself Truthfully

Below is the most important image in this book—your competitive minds, both of them:

(L) Your Little Dog mind—the **"I can't"** thinker: doubting confused, and panicked.

(R) Your Big Dog mind—the **"I can"** thinker: confident, focused, and composed.

Get Real! Look at "both" of your competitive minds truthfully. Know with clarity, in each game situation, whether you're doubtful, tentative, or confident.

Grappling with both of your *competitive minds* is how to conquer doubt and become a confident competitor. The first step is the most difficult—*get real*.

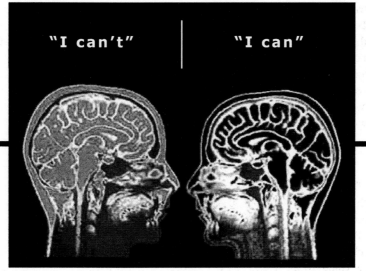

"I can't"   "I can"

Artist Unknown

"Whether you think you can or you can't you're probably right."

— Henry Ford

Above: Rio Mesa's Sergio Ordonez, left, looks on as Scott Beckman of Camarillo controls the ball with a leaping kick at Camarillo High School. Photo by Staff

Did I lose you there? The majority of us walk around *looking* all confident and powerful, but actuality that's only a projection of an image we've mentally created. A lot of us are trying to trick ourselves (and others) into believing we're Big Dogs, but as soon as a real challenge presents itself we crash, because our confidence is founded on fantasy and we can't take fantasy into battle.

The sooner we look ourselves squarely in the competitive face and see who really comes out when we step onto the field, either our Little Dog or our Big Dog, the sooner we'll be able to manage how our minds work. This is how Little Dogs find their Big Dog and how Big Dogs calm themselves down.

First, we have to be truthful about being who we really are and how we mentally react in competition. If we're Little Dogs, we need to admit that, so we can motivate ourselves to find our Big Dog.

Understanding our *true competitive confidence* is what Big Dog Visualization is all about. It helps mere athletes transform into confident, successful competitors. To repeat: for some of us this is a difficult journey because we refuse to face who we truly are in a competitive environment.

Many athletes limit their training to one element, the physical, because it's the easiest to understand. But, to be successful competitors, we need to consistently work on two elements—the body AND the mind.

Hard Work

It is generally accepted in the athletic community, especially at the youth and high school level, that hard work is the cure-all for everything. Respectfully, I disagree.

I've known many athletes who worked as hard as anyone, on and off the field, but when it's game time, they emotionally fall apart. If hard work were the only ticket necessary to win gold, many more non-champions would be champions.

It's a misconception that hard physical work translates into mental toughness or mental dominance. The lines have been blurred.

Yes, it's true; athletes must develop a work ethic that many people will not commit to; athletes have to work hard and sacrifice. Yes, there is a certain mental element that goes along with building commitment, work tolerance, and oxygen exchange capability (conditioning). But that isn't the mental side of competing, that's the mental side of not being a physical wimp.

In weightlifting, doing rep after rep, set after set, day after day is a "mental thing," but that's not mental toughness. That's training hard. Being mentally tough in a competitive environment is an entirely different planet, totally unlike training or practice.

The majority of young athletes could train until they're blue in the face, but as they walk into the stadium would still lay-an-egg, because they haven't learned how to control their fears or focus their minds as they stare down a worthy opponent.

Coaches: Help your players become competitors. Encourage them to program their minds along with working their bodies, so they can win the confidence battle. It will immediately elevate your team's overall competitive intensity. They will be able to compete at a winning level almost instantly.

When training, it's much easier to focus on the body because we can see it. It's easy to see the body sweat, it's easy to see excellent physical skills, and it's easy to see well-executed ball handling. In contrast, it's much harder to see someone's mind working, or not working. But, if we train ourselves to "see" mental confidence, it's as easy as evaluating a great shot, a disciplined defense or a perfect pass.

The trouble is, we can't lie about the pass—we either put the ball where we wanted to or we didn't. But, unlike that good or bad pass, the mind is hidden. Plus, most of us have a tendency to lie about our emotions and confidence because we think we'll be perceived as weak—a Little Dog tendency.

The primary point here is: the first step to finding your Big Dog deep inside is being truthful with yourself.

Physical Toughness

Physical toughness – the will to train hard, play banged-up, broken and fatigued – is a part of mental toughness, but overcoming physical pain has little to do with competitive confidence. The physical punishment required to practice like a madman is why so many kids bail, but enduring physical difficulties alone does not create mental competitive dominance.

"You'll never find 'the zone' with your Little Dog in control—worried, shaking, and doubtful."

Don't misunderstand me. I'm not saying that monster hard work is not a vital ingredient to being a successful player, it definitely is. But that's only half of the equation. We also need the mental skills of a Big Dog competitor to walk out of state or national competitions as champions.

At state and nationals all the top ranked players have worked hard … physically. It's the athletes who also work hard mentally who take home gold.

Mental Toughness

Mental toughness includes being able to deal with the harshness of self-evaluation—the internal psychology of how one views oneself. Not feels— VIEWS. And there is a big difference. **One is opinion, the other is reality.**

Mental evaluation is far scarier territory than physical evaluation, especially in the 21st Century. Why? Because a low percentage of our society hold themselves accountable> Apprenticeship does not exist and everyone thinks they're entitled to success without effort and discipline. Few people want to work for greatness. To openly look at ourselves with any level of realism is like pulling teeth—we run and hide.

Above: Cathedral's Kofi Amoako, left, and Minnechaug's Benjamin Bradford vie for a head ball during the second half at Szot Park in Chicopee. Photo by Christopher Evans/Union News

Make sense? Most of us, not just teens, do not want to see ourselves for who we really are inside. But as athletes, if we want to be able to control our emotions we have to know our minds and how our minds work.

Mental dominance is being able to see our fears and doubt, admit them and being able to overcome them. It's a process which must be practiced before it can be mastered.

As a world-class competitor, it's been my experience that *truth with oneself is where the power lies.* When we get out of our own way and channel the tremendous mental power that we all have, and allow our personality, physical skills, and hard work to take over; it's an incredible experience we never forget. This is often referred to as "the zone." It almost feels effortless and to achieve it takes a combination of both physical *and* mental skills. We all have the capability; we just have to develop it, to realize it.

I guarantee this; you will never find the zone with your Little Dog in control—worried, shaking and doubtful.

Mental-Evaluation

First, let's create a comparison to get a clear picture. We could easily do a physical evaluation, correct? I could travel to any team in the county and hand out a physical evaluation sheet for each player that had a 1–3 rating in three categories: technique, endurance and power. If everyone gave their *truthful* opinion and the evaluations were averaged, it would provide a pretty accurate picture of each player's physical capability. Right? No big deal. As athletes, we're constantly sizing each other up. We know who is getting stronger, who's looking leaner, who's getting quicker and who's acting like a wimp. Those variables change from week to week. We keep up-to-date mental data on our group's physical capability. It's just what we athletes do.

What about confidence and heart? Actually, I think we do the same thing, maybe a little less consciously. But, we do know who is confident and who is timid, who will crack under pressure and who won't, who is aggressive and who is passive. Just like the physical variables, those confidence and heart variables change from minute-to-minute, day-to-day, and week-to-week.

For example, if I asked everyone on a team who was the strongest, I'd instantly hear a name. If I asked who had the best technique, I might hear a couple of names. But, if I asked who was the toughest, it would get quiet. Even though we know who the toughest is, that's not something we're going to quickly acknowledge. If I asked who mentally had the most confidence, same thing—quiet. But, if I asked who choked the most, BAM! Names would come out. We can nail those guys.

Do you see the parallels I am drawing? Guys, it's more important to be truthful with yourself and to know the strengths of your mind than the strengths of your body. I'll take a *mental giant* over a physical powerhouse any day. Once you pop a hole in the powerhouse's illusion of his physical superiority, he's done. He'll crash and burn. That's the main thing Little Dogs don't understand about attitude—it's all in our minds. *We create attitude.* You know the saying, "The bigger they are the harder they fall." Where do you think that comes from?

Mental evaluation is tougher than physical evaluation. Our minds work like blenders. When we add emotion it's like pushing the puree button—the lid flies off and excuses splatter everywhere.

Take emotion out of the equation. It's like taking taste out of fueling—it doesn't belong. *Emotion and clear, unbiased mental-evaluation are like oil and water, they don't belong together.*

It's much easier for coaches to physically evaluate their teams than to psychologically evaluate them. Here is a general way to evaluate a team. Physical: technique, endurance, and power. Mental: confidence and heart. Use a 1-3 rating in each category and after compiling each individual player's rating, you've got a team rating.

If a team's confidence and heart rating didn't average at least a 2.7, mental practice should be long and hard until they bring their mental score up. Then, the team can walk into any stadium in the country blazing with confi-

BIG-DOG™
Visualization

Program your mind so you can step-up, believe, and score with confidence.

During big-play opportunities, when your team needs you most, use **Big Dog Visualization** to change Little Dog doubt into Big Dog dominance. Deliver the level of play you're capable of—fierce, game winning play.

"I can't"
**Little Dog
thinking.**

"I can"
**Big Dog
thinking.**

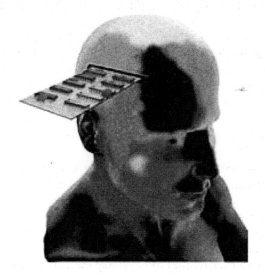

Artist Unknown

**"Most battles are won before they
are fought."**

— Sun Tzu

Above: Player unknown. Photo source neptunesoccer.com

dence instead of projecting arrogance. I've seen this positive transformation take place within individuals many times and a soccer team is no more than a group of individuals, who are committed and focused on a collective outcome.

Mental-evaluation is similar to any touchy subject—once we bring it out in the open, it's not as touchy as we think. Evaluating confidence and heart is the same thing. Once we openly talk about it and don't run away from it, we can start to work on it, *which is how we improve.*

Projecting

We all project. It's how we get our personalities out of ourselves and into the environment. We manipulate the projection to get what we want in specific situations. If you think about it, you know exactly what I'm talking about.

The attitude and personality you project when you're sitting at the dinner table with your family is very different than the attitude you project when you're hanging with your buddies.

We control those different outward projections, whether we realize it or not. We learn how to do this very early in life, and, as our personalities grow, our projections multiply and change.

Undisciplined Big Dogs and poser Little Dogs often make the mistake at competitions of constantly projecting, which takes a tremendous amount of energy.

On a day-to-day basis Big Dogs project their physical superiority and aggressive tendencies within their social groups. This is how they establish their "alphadom." But, at a competition it's a total waste of energy, and worse, it's distracting.

Staring down or mugging opposing players, projecting the tractor-beam stare across the field is a complete waste. It's a Little Dog trying to act like a Big Dog. You're diverting valuable energy and concentration into the outer environment. You're actually putting on a display *rather then preparing to dominate your opponent and leave him staring at the ground wondering what just happened.*

Weightlifters can be the worst at this—yelling, slapping, huffing and puffing. What do they think they're doing, intimidating the weights? I don't think so. Or some might say, "That's what gets me up." I don't think so. Bottom line, it's an outward display of fear. They're scared to death and they don't know how to channel their emotions. They release that pent-up, valuable emotional energy all over the arena, which is both rookie behavior and a tremendous energy drain.

As a competitor I used to enjoy watching all those goofballs going through their displays of fear. They gave me a competitive advantage by exhausting themselves.

Don't project—at all—it's worthless. Harness and focus your emotional energy. *Dominating is not about acting; it's about doing.*

Harness & Control

To me the word "harness" implies that we already have it. We don't have to get it or develop it. We just have to control and channel it. We all have incredible mental power that must be harnessed and controlled or it will destroy us.

I can say that with such conviction, because we're all equipped with the ability to, if necessary, fight with extreme intensity. It's a basic survival capability. Just because some of us choose to shrivel-up and mentally submit when we're scared, doesn't mean that we don't have incredible mental intensity. It just means we choose not to use it, which is a HUGE distinction.

Harnessing and controlling emotions is the key to a player's competitive success. The main point is you have it and it's your choice whether you use it or it uses you.

Open Minds

"Minds are like parachutes, they only work when they're open."
(Sir James Dewar, Scientist)

I encourage all you Dogs to open your minds and be truthful with your-selves. A great discovery lies ahead—seeing your true competitive mindset. And once you've grappled with and mastered it, you'll have your Dogs on a tight leash, and high-level competitive confidence on command.

"Don't just look for mistakes you made physically, look and identify your competitive psychology: Were you scared, tentative, or confident?"

It is so critically important for all of you to realize that you already have tremendous mental intensity, so learn how to focus, get out of your own way, show some teeth, and let your Big Dog out.

The Process

Now we get to the nuts and bolts of looking truthfully at your perform-ance, your two Dogs, and how they really react under pressure.

Again, this is rough territory guys. For a lot of us, this is when all sorts of mental blocks go up and excuses start erupting, which is natural. We live in a defensive society; everyone is always blaming someone else, and making excuses for themselves. But, let me tell you, every champion has to go though this personal evaluation in order to genuinely be confident in battle. As competitors, we have to know ourselves in order to control ourselves.

Hopefully, you have some video of past performances. We're going to focus on two totally opposite outcomes. The first tape is when you were a Little Dog; you were scared, intimidated, and choked. The second tape should be of a performance when you were a Big Dog; you were confident, you executed well and you felt like a champion.

How did you just react internally to even thinking about watching the first video, when you choked? Did you get a lump in your throat? Did you

Above: Easthampton's Drew Nalewanski, left, gets tied up with Northampton's Miles Montgomery-Butler as they grapple for possession. The teams played to a 2-all tie in the Holley Division matchup. Photo by Mieke Zuiderweg/Union News

get a little nervous? Feel a little weird? You probably don't even want to watch it. Well guess what, get over it and take a look.

Now, sit down with someone you trust and respect, who can talk with you about how and why you felt the way you did. For you young guys, it should be someone older, with some competitive experience. First, review video #1—the choked performance. What is your internal reaction? How do you handle watching yourself choking? Are you embarrassed? Are you hiding emotionally? Making excuses? Or are you being truthful and learning something? Does watching that real experience shrink you or motivate you? Take a serious look at your Little Dog in action. Don't look for flawed technique or your physical mistakes. Look at your Little Dog factor, your lack of confidence and execution. **Ask yourself questions.** Why were you so shook? There are real reasons. We don't have a meltdown just because. Have a meaningful discussion with your trusted friend and get to the bottom of why you choked.

Then review video #2, when you were a Big Dog—when you dominated. Analyze your Big Dog factor with the same questions. Why were you confident, and all the rest? Break the reasons down. "I don't know" is mentally lazy and lame. Get to the bottom of why you felt confident. Be able to explain the reasons "why" in both performances, so you can clearly understand your competitive mindset.

Trust me here. Getting real with yourself is the first step toward improving. Again, don't look for mistakes you made physically, look and identify your psychology. Why were you scared or confident, and to what degree?

Are you starting to see how this works? It's really simple when we're willing to be real with ourselves. Once we go through the process a few (hundred) times, we start to see a pattern develop: scared, tentative, or confident. Each, of course has degrees, but we find ourselves in one of those three categories the majority of the time.

Big Dog Visualization DVDs

Now, it's time to create some mental Big Dog Visualization DVDs. One for each of our emotional categories: scared, tentative, and confident.

No doubt you guys are starting to see how this works, but I will walk you though the process anyhow. Remember, if you're not completely truthful with yourself, none of this will work.

Little dog Scared DVD: Just like the process I described previous, for evaluating the videos of past Little Dog performances, mentally go back to one or two more game situations when you were scared out of your mind, when you could not even think. Now this is the important part. Clearly document what sent you into Little Dog mode. Was it the other team's reputation? Was your opponent a knock you off your feet tackler? Or all the pressure was on you to make the winning goal? Or was it a title game? Watch yourself in those different situations, and mentally rewind the experience. Document very clearly what happened from the first thought that tweaked you, because when you mentally rewind and look, you're getting a real-time view of one of your competitive minds—your scared Little Dog. Once you've remembered several of the scared experiences, and have analyzed the reasons why you were tweaked, burn those experiences and feelings on your mental Scared DVD.

Little dog Tentative DVD: This is very similar to the Scared DVD, but not as intense. Most likely, you'll be tentative more often in game situations than truly scared. Go back to a couple of games when you were tentative, when you hesitated, and clearly document why. Why were you feeling uncertain? Give yourself specific, real reasons. Don't guess—know. Because what you're replaying in your mind is not a fantasy, it is a real experience of your tentative Little Dog. Once you've remembered a couple of game experiences and have analyzed the reasons why you were tentative, mentally burn those experiences and feelings on your mental Tentative DVD.

Above: New Dorp's James Ponpon looks on as St. Peter's Vincent Impertrice heads a pass. Photo by Hilton Flores/Staten Island Advance

Big Dog Confident DVD: This is the fun DVD. Make sure you have many, as in dozens, of confident game experiences recorded. And each time you have a new one, record it as well—the more current the better. Use the same process as above. Ask yourself questions and understand why you were confident. Be very clear about which experiences you burn to your Confident DVD. You will use this DVD over and over and over. Why? Because the Confident DVD is the one you will insert in your head (figuratively speaking) when you're scared or tentative.

It is vital that you understand the full spectrum of your competitive emotions: scared, tentative and confident.

Defense late in the game: Everybody gets tired. But late in the game one goal can make the difference between winning a championship or going home empty handed. Staying focused and confident is doubly important for defense, if you hesitate or letdown, you can quickly give up position. If you don't truly believe you can stop your opponent, you letdown emotionally. If their striker has been beating you more than you've been stopping him; if their midfielder is a brutal tackler and you're tired of the battle; and if their keeper seems to stop everything, don't let it break your spirit. Late in the game, when it's a real battle, that's when you need to keep your spirits high. It's when to mentally focus on the positive, not the negative. Plug in your Confident DVD to believe in yourself. Don't letdown emotionally. Late in the game is when players become champions. Let your Big Dog out, conquer your doubt, and make BIG-Plays when your team needs them most.

Insert Disk

The photo on page 69 is probably the most important photo in this book. Those are our two minds: our Little Dog mind and our Big Dog mind—our scared "I can't" psychology and our confident "I can" psychology. Those two opposing emotions are constantly battling for control.

Now review the picture on page 75. That's how we have to think when we're scared or tentative, we're reprogramming our competitive minds. We're *replacing* doubt with confidence by understanding why we're going

**Above: The Wolve's bench.   Photo source PlymouthPictures.com
Note: On the bench, work your mind to stay confident.**

into a meltdown, and then telling our Little Dog where to go and focusing on real experiences when we were confident, to convince ourselves we can believe in our Big Dog mindset. The reason? We've done it before; been there, did that.

Are you starting to make the connection? When we're truthful with ourselves we can see our competitive minds work—both of them—then with Big Dog Visualization we edit or dismiss our weaknesses and confirm our confidence, which translates into mental dominance. Mentally reprogramming ourselves is as simple as inserting a disk, but in order for the reprogramming to work, *we have to be truthful, so we can believe.*

The next step is early meltdown detection; to know when our Little Dog is taking over, before he has us sniveling in the corner. In game situations, it's very important to be constantly assessing where you're at on the Doubt Meter. If you're climbing about a 2.0, you need to be able to quickly reason with yourself, so you can talk yourself down, and then coach yourself up. Ask yourself why your stomach is in knots and why you don't believe in yourself? See your Big Dog come out and chase your Little Dog into submission. Create visions of real experiences that will help you see WHY you can believe in yourself—because you can. Eventually, with practice, you'll learn how to detect and control your Little Dog "I can't" psychology, by replacing it with BIG-Dog "I can" psychology.

Remember, competing successfully is all about attitude, and attitude is entirely in your mind.

The entire point of the Big Dog Visualization process is to vividly see yourself emotionally crashing, talking yourself down, and then coaching yourself back up. The first step is key: Don't deny it. Then, by purposefully taking a clear look at why you were in a meltdown, you can recover, and then dominate.

No matter what happens, no matter where you are, no matter whom you're up against, you have a similar experience on either your Scared or Tentative DVD. That's why you have those DVDs – so you can remember having a similar experience. You know? The 'been there, did that,' frame of mind. It's old news and nothing to be afraid of. Now you insert your Confident DVD to bring yourself back to reality: **You're a stud, so believe in yourself.**

I mentioned in Chapter 1 that visualization isn't about the rewards; it's about the battle. And even though I'm pretty certain you now understand why, let me clarify: visualizing rewards is OK—if it's at the end of a battle session. If you want to create your DVDs so that once you control your Little Dog and your Big Dog comes out and dominates, then you see yourself making the perfect pass or game winning goal, the crowd erupts, and you and your team are holding the championship trophy over your heads—that's all good.

Anywhere

Once you've conquered your fear of looking at yourself truthfully, and you've created your Big Dog Visualization DVDs, you can use the replacement technique anytime, anywhere. If you're lying in bed the night before a big game and feel yourself getting a little tweaked, you know what to do. Plug in your Confident DVD. There are so many situations where you can use this technique: If it's your first year on varsity and you're feeling a little intimidated; if you're off at a camp, and matched up with some great talent; if you just made a mistake, late in a big game; plug in your Confident DVD and replace feelings of doubt and intimidation, with memories of success and accomplishment.

No matter where you're at, no matter what situation it is, now you have the technique to develop the mental skills to successfully manage your competitive emotions.

Patience

Patience competitors. Developing Big Dog Visualization is a process that takes time and practice. It's just like developing a physical skill you had to practice over and over until you got it right—until the skill felt natural, and eventually you could use it at will. Big Dog Visualization is the same thing.

Give yourself time and be diligent about practicing *replacement* visualization. In no time you'll know how to subdue your Little Dog and control your emotions. Big Dog Visualization will help you replace doubt with confidence, so you can deliver the level of play you're capable of—clutch, game winning play.

SUMMARY

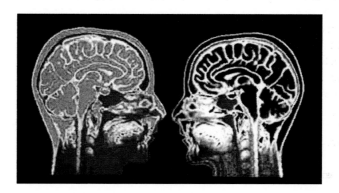

- Program your mind to believe in yourself.

- Get real.

- Truthfully look your competitive minds square in the face; know whether you're scared, tentative, or confident.

- Be able to replace doubt and intimidation with confidence and success anytime, anywhere.

- Don't project; it's worthless.

- Watch your confident DVDs to replace Little Dog doubt into Big Dog dominance.

- Be patient. Big Dog Visualization takes practice.

"*Muster the courage to look your competitive minds square in the face. In no time you'll be able to manage your competitive emotions under pressure. Be persistent with building your Big Dog Confident DVD collection, so you can believe.*"

— Steve Knight

Chapter 6

THE BATTLE • Composure

Now it's time to play some soccer. All of the preparation is behind you. You're chilling in the locker room—waiting. You feel confident, but uncertain. You don't know how sharp you'll be until you step on to the field and take the first pass. Now the real battle begins—the confidence battle—the battle over composure.

Transitions

The battle over composure is fought in the transitions. As we move mentally and physically from our causal everyday life, to our intensely focused

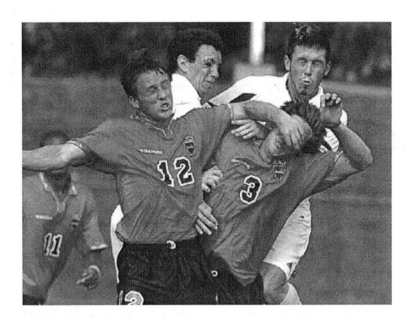

"What the mind and imagination believe the human body can achieve."

— Unknown Author

Above: Minnechaug's Jeff Snyder, left, and Cathedral's Bryan Wo-jtowicz collide on an attempted header. Minnechaug won the Smith Division showdown, 2-1. Photo by Union-News

Left: IU Soccer Adidas Classic. Photo by Paul B. Riley/IU Athletics

competitive life, we go through transitions. From home, to the stadium, from chilling on the couch, to scrambling for position, from subbing-out briefly, to focusing on a critical free kick. There are short transitions and long transitions, easy transitions and hard transitions. If these examples seem too drastic, that casual and competitive are two different worlds— perfect—because they are. The transition from an affectionate family member to an intense competitor *is that drastic.*

Above: Bloomfield's Carlos Borja, center, tries to get to the ball before Randolph's Oleg Lejnin, left, and Paul Kusik. Photo by Christopher Barth/Star-Ledger

Right: Regis' Pat Bugas (5) cuts off St. Joseph by-the-Sea's John Tardy's. Photo by Hilton Flores/Staten Island Advance

As you pull into the parking lot at an away game, get off the bus, hit the locker room, and then take the field, you're going through a series of transitions. Even though you settle down emotionally after the first few minutes of a game, you still go through many transitions as the game progresses. It's a constant roller coaster: focus, then chill—focus, then chill. Each cycle from focused to unfocused, and then back to focused, is a transition.

The majority of the time our Little Dog takes over during the transitions, which is when we talk ourselves out of what we can do and into what we can't do. The transition is when most of us go nuts, meltdown emotionally and lose our composure.

Example: The time between warm-ups and the opening kick-off can be a time when we either enjoy the intensity of the moment and get pumped

about competing, or we emotionally crash under the pressure and get off to a stumbling, rocky start.

Without being conscious of the transitions, how can we go from being mentally relaxed to competitively focused? We can't. In order to move from one place to another, either physically or mentally, there must be a transition. The transition is a weird place, both mentally and emotionally; it's where our fantasies meet our convictions. Meaning: it's where our true competitive mind reveals itself. Some of us rise up, out position the defense and make the play with confidence, while others stumble and fall because they don't believe in themselves.

During those minutes, hours or days before intense competitions, much of our mental/emotional energy is spent in that transition zone between causal and competitive—battling self-doubt and negative "what if" outcomes. It's a continuous and repetitive pre-game process. The main transition is when we get close to actually stepping on to the field, not just thinking about it. That's when our Big Dog needs to come out and dominate our thinking. Successfully managing the transitions that lead into pressure transitions is when we need the mental skills of a seasoned competitor to come out a winner.

Patience & Focus

As I said before, there are many transitions before and during each and every game, and one of the keys to successfully maintaining composure is realizing that games are hurry-up and wait situations. Waiting starts as soon as you get to the stadium and there's a lot more waiting during the game. Warm-ups (stretching and skill drills) can be times of transition, where you get distracted by all the pre-game commotion; it can steal your competitive edge. Then, during the game, whether you're on the field, the bench, or the ball is away from your immediate area, you need to stay competitively focused and not allow yourself to get distracted. Those brief downtimes are when we mentally wander and lose our competitive focus. The downtimes are when patience and focus are critical to maintaining a competitive mindset.

Generally, the underlying theme for successfully staying composed during big-play transitions is patience and focus. **And the secret ingredient is discipline.** Discipline is what glues those elements together. The discipline required at a major championship "away" game is probably the hardest discipline to master—especially for teens. Not only do you guys want to run around all night getting into mischief (chasing cheerleaders), you also want to plot and explore all day long.

Here comes the dad/coach stern-faced finger-pointing speech: get a grip! Why are you there? Why have you worked so hard? Is it party time or game time? Why end up performing poorly because you indulged your pleasure interests? Why not battle like a focused Big Dog all the way to the last play of the championship game? Well? Make positive decisions that propel you towards your dream, not leave you sitting in dejection.

Sticking with straight talk: Stay focused and concentrate on what's important. Don't blow it once you get to the playoffs. Plotting and indulging in social activities diverts your focus and lowers your competitive intensity. Like it or not competing in the playoffs, at an away stadium, is NOT a full-on girl chasing social adventure. Winning a multi-game state tournament

Championship
Pre-Game Mindset

The championship games are when you and your team get a shot at the dream, and it's when many players come unglued.

Develop a pre-game mindset to stabilize your emotions.

Chill: Previous to arriving at the stadium, just chill.

Disconnect: Before suiting-up, mentally disconnect from the environment and your teammates. Close your eyes, rest, think of all the great plays you made during the season.

Stay Calm: As you hit the field, keep that special emotional energy inside, save it for the game—when it's all on the line.

Visualize: Use Big Dog Visualization to be confident, not doubtful. Keep your mind in an "I can" mindset.

Game Mode: Keep your focus narrow, control your emotions, and believe in yourself—**CONCENTRATE!**

Above: IU NCAA champions. Photo by Paul Riley/IU Athletics

"If winning isn't everything, why do they keep score?"

— Vince Lombardi

takes an extraordinary level of concentration and conviction. The reality is: you can't have it all.

For all of you scammers who are smiling and thinking that you can have it all—that you can party, chase girls, and still perform at a superior level—sorry, you're in fantasyland.

This point is so important, let's look at it from a different angle. For many of you, traveling with your team is a new experience and emotionally you treat it like some sort of vacation. I've seen the distractions at state and nationals derail many would-be champions, because they lost their competitive focus and decided (unconsciously) to indulge themselves socially. I encourage you to keep your head on straight, discipline yourself, and conserve your energy for the game. In other words, when you're off the field, don't deviate from your Game Mode perspective. If your focus wanders before the final whistle, of the last game, it is likely that you will suffer some sort of negative consequences.

This isn't a karma thing; it's a focus thing. The mind can only do one thing at a time. Switching from casual mode to Game Mode isn't easy for most of us. While we do have to put our laser-beam focus on pause a lot of the time, during the playoffs, we have to keep at least one eye on the prize 24/7. Mentally wandering, i.e., fully engaging social activities is a big mistake.

Trust me, during the playoffs is not the time to goof around. Multi-day tournaments are too draining to waste valuable time and energy on social distractions. The mind and habits of a Big Dog competitor are focused, confident and determined. Try not to fall into the Little Dog trap, mistaking an away playoff game for Disneyland or some sort of group vacation. Get a grip guys; it's a competition. At playoff games, especially the championship game, you need to be the most patient, be the most focused, and have the most discipline. Yeah, have fun, but don't forget why you're there—you are there to compete, and win.

Timing

As soon as the Ref blows the whistle, the game is on and the emotional roller coaster lurches forward. Your mind races and your stomach twists. The negative "what if" mental battle goes into full gear, especially if it's a big game and there are high expectations for you to perform.

The type of timing we're discussing here is not about any one play or a great shot, great pass, or great defensive position; it's about the flow of the game, and mentally transitioning from relaxed to focused.

As we've discussed, staying intensely focused all of the time is almost impossible; so paying attention to the flow of the game and how you fit into that flow is vital to being confident when big-play opportunities present

Above: Players unknown. Photo source neptunesoccer.com

themselves. In other words, knowing when to turn your laser-beam focus off, is just as important as knowing when to turn it on.

Starters, when you're getting a breather, disengage the game for a minute or two to give your mind and emotions a rest. Role players, yeah, do some game watching, but take care of your emotions and turn your laser-beam focus off, so you'll be ready to give 100% when it's your turn to hit the field.

The bottom line about timing is learning how to stay connected with the flow of the game to better manage the 20 or 30 times you'll transition from relaxed to intensely focused each game.

Above: Kolo Goshi, No. 18 - senior from Kpada, Nigeria. Photo by
Jim Veneman

Right: Players unknown. First Colony Soccer Club. Photo by Steve
Matthews

Sideline Dynamics

Wow! The sidelines. It can either be your best friend or your worst enemy. Everything can distract you: intense coaches, freaked out teammates
and too much time to focus on the wrong things. At times, learning how to
mentally deal with the dynamics of the sidelines can be more critical than
the dynamics on the field. The sidelines are where we either emotionally
coach ourselves up or tear ourselves down. The sidelines are a breeding
ground for emotionally instability.

The transitions on the sidelines are when many of you emotionally
crash. Every time you sub-out, make sure you're using your Confidence
Routines to stay composed, so you're ready to hit the field minutes later.
While on the sidelines, your Confidence Routines are what will help you
recover mentally and stay connected with the flow of the game. The specifics of how you handle the sidelines are different for each of you.

Personally, I'm the type that needs to disconnect from everyone around
me, at least for a few minutes, because I'm easily distracted. It's not that I
don't want to support my teammates; it's because making a positive transition takes me a little longer. Other competitors can flip the switch and go

from casual to Game Mode in an instant. My mental process is not so quick and requires a little more concentration.

Each of us has his own way of getting focused or unfocused. Some of us can handle more distractions than others. Example: Some people can read effectively in a crowed, noisy room. For me that's impossible.

Chatty teammates, or teammates who are melting down emotionally throwing up all over the place are the worst; it drives me nuts—doubt can be contagious. My simple technique to keep others' doubt eruptions off me, and to narrow my focus, is to put a towel over my head for a few minutes to disconnect and center myself. Somehow, be able to close your eyes, hear your favorite music, and imagine whatever will take you to a clam, restful place. For those of you who find talking relaxing, make sure you hook up with teammates who have a similar competitive style.

Some of you need to get a little angry and pace around in order to pump yourself up. The bottom-line is: do what you need to do. There are many ways to get to the promised land of Big Dog self-confidence, and all of the different competitive styles are why I call it "sideline dynamics." There is a lot going on and everyone is in close proximity with each other. You can't escape your teammates' energies, so it's very important to figure out what works best for you, and then to make sure you put yourself in the position to make it happen. In other words, don't let the dynamics of the sidelines take you out of your competitive mindset. Take control and use your Confidence Routines to stay focused, composed, and confident.

"I've seen the distractions at state derail many would be champions, because they lost their competitive focus."

Critical Minutes

During the critical minutes of a game is when your true confidence gets tested—your "actual" confidence, not your fantasy confidence. Even though everything is happening at an incredibly fast pace, have the presence of mind to know where you're at on the Doubt Meter. If you're a little lethargic and distracted, you had better tune in, and get yourself pumped-up. If you're getting tweaked, plug in your Big Dog confident DVD, focus on your strengths, calm your doubts, and breathe. Did I mention breathe? I mean breathe. Oxygen will help you manage the adrenaline that is dumping into your blood stream from the excitement of competing under pressure.

Let's pause a moment to talk about adrenaline. Powerful stuff. Without getting technical, adrenaline's bottom-line is: RUN! When we feel threatened, glands dump adrenaline into our blood stream, which quickly increases our physical and mental capability. During the critical minutes is usually where an adrenaline dump happens.

There are a couple of significant adrenaline rush side effects that you need to be aware of. The first and worst is when too much adrenaline is dumped at once. It's usually caused by genuine doubt or extreme fear—our Little Dog is freaking. A monster adrenaline rush can make us feel nauseous

Above: St. Francis' Clark Sanchez-Figueras and Westlake's Brian Jones go for the ball. Photo by James Glover II/Star staff

(yep, some puke), lightheaded, unfocused, physically weak, and can cause all sorts of other negative side effects. Coming down from an adrenaline rush can leave us feeling lethargic and tired—sort of a letdown.

The way out of a monster adrenaline rush is oxygen and concentration; breathe and talk yourself down. Control it, don't let it control you. There is more adrenaline where that came from, which is a good thing, so don't freak-out. Compose yourself emotionally and get back in control. So when the play hinges on you, you'll be focused and ready to execute.

Most world-class athletes have learned how to control adrenaline rushes, but it takes many years of high-level competition to really master adrenaline. At the very least, know that an adrenaline rush feels edgy, nervous and weird. Breathe; it's a good thing.

Downtime Transitions: *Knowing how to properly disengage and deal with transitions is essential to maintaining composure. It might seem that when the ball is on the opposite side of the field you can relax for a moment, but that's not the case. The ball moves at lightning speed. The ball can be in one place one second and at your feet the next. What does that mean? You have to be ready. Even though you might not be intensely focused when the ball is out of your area, you have to be ready without hesitation when the opportunity appears, if you want to make clutch plays. Being able to turn on laser beam concentration on and off in an instant is one of the keys to making clutch plays when they're needed most. Knowing how to relax and disengage when you're off the field, maximizing your bench time, is how you'll be able to step-up and execute late in the game. So, when you're off the field know what's happening on the field, but emotionally disengage so you can keep yourself composed for upcoming pressure situations. Late in the game, the best way to have the mental energy to keep up the attack is to rest your emotions during the downtime transitions.*

Back to the critical minutes.

Every play is important; whether defensive or offensive, but some are clutch—when your team needs you to step-up and really deliver. Those are the times when you prove whether you're just a player or a clutch competitor. The critical minutes are when laser beam focus is essential; it's a transition from being partly in the game mentally, to full on lock-tone on the target. The critical minutes is when many players let their negative emotions take over, and they get lost in "what if" possibilities—mental chatter that is totally unproductive.

Cowboy-Up
It Ain't Easy

Uncertainty, adversity, injury, intimidation; it doesn't matter; a "clutch" player looks difficulty square in the face and overcomes.

In other words, it ain't gonna be easy. COWBOY-UP!

All season long, in every game, one way or another; it comes down to proving yourself. Are you a poser or a player?

Decide. Then live with it.

Cowboy Unknown. Photo by David Huber

"It's not how big you are, it's how big you play."

— Unknown

Example: As you and your teammates move the ball down the field, you're either focused and confident, concentrating on the dynamics of the flow, feeling the momentum, or mentally scattered thinking about negative outcomes: What if this guy beats me again; what if I hesitate; what if I turn the ball over? Then, if your thoughts remain negative you see all sorts of undesirable consequences: you let your team down, you don't get the scholarship, and life ends as you know it. Those, and many other variations of that kind of thinking are negative "what if" possibilities.

"With your Big Dog in control, you'll be able to play at the level your capable of—full on, attacking, game winning play."

Now that you have a better understanding of your two competitive minds, I bet you know which one of your dogs is doing the negative "what if" thinking. Exactly: Your Little Dog. Your Big Dog isn't interested in the negative; if your Big Dog engages in "what if" thinking, it's going to be positive; seeing yourself confidently attacking your opponent, taking the ball away, making the shot, winning the game, getting the scholarship, and your team holding the championship trophy over your heads.

During the critical minutes, use the mental skills you've been working on to calm your Little Dog down, so your Big Dog can dominate your thinking. With your Big Dog in control, you'll be able to play at the level you're capable of—full on, attacking, game winning play.

New Opportunity

Stepping onto a soccer field in any situation, let alone during big games, is clearly an emotional challenge. If you were strapped with a heart rate indicator and a blood pressure monitor, you would be amazed. Your heart is pounding and your blood pressure is soaring. This is one of the reasons why I have such a healthy respect for those who love to compete. Running full speed, crashing shoulders and knocking heads, takes both guts and grace. But stealing the ball and driving it forward takes more than just guts, it takes emotional confidence.

Above: Player unknown. Photo source: neptunesoccer.com

Remember this guys: sound physical skills are just the first step. Obviously a critical first step, but physical mechanics are not what scores points; your confidence is what allows you to use your great mechanics. If you don't have confidence, the best mechanics in the world are worthless.

NOTE: If you're connecting with the techniques and methods I'm teaching throughout this book, at this point you should be mentally seeing how to handle yourself on the field. If you're not, don't worry, just go back and read chapters one through five again so you can really burn those concepts into your mind. Your great speed and footwork didn't happen overnight; so understanding your minds, both of them, and how to manage doubt and fear under pressure is no different. It takes practice and patience.

Each time the ball is in your area, it's a new opportunity, so look to the future, don't dwell on the past. If you have your Little Dog under control, and your Big Dog is bearing his teeth, you're going to succeed, because you're good and you believe in yourself.

Getting Behind

When your team gets behind, don't emotionally letdown or freak out. Just like any other pressure packed situation, control it, don't let it control you. Take a deep breath, take control of the rhythm, and see your opponent and the field through your composed Big Dog mindset. Focus on previous clutch situations, don't hesitate, and attack, attack, attack. If you let yourself get emotionally desperate, you won't perform to the best of your abilities. Getting behind, if you think about it, at some point, is almost a natural course of most big game situations. So make adjustments, look to the next play, and believe.

Finals

If you've made it to that state or national finals, you and your teammates are obviously doing a lot of things right. The primary concerns now, more than ever, are avoiding distractions and staying emotionally balanced.

Warning: It's not time to celebrate just because you've made it to the finals. This is a bad move guys, and I've seen it happen too many times; don't release all of that pent-up emotional energy.

Here's the situation: you and your teammates have been committed for months. You're in the finals and it feels great. One more game and the season is over. One more game and it could be the team dog pile in the middle of the field. One more game and you and your teammates could be holding the championship trophy high over your heads. Getting to the finals is a tremendous accomplishment, and naturally you feel like celebrating.

But wait! Get a grip.

**Above: Daniel Mullan celebrates his winning goal. Photo source
www.teamtalkmag.com**

Oops ... first, I should ask you about your dream. Is your dream to be a
state champion or just make it to the finals? If it's just to make it to the finals,
go celebrate. If it's to battle hard and win the championship, put your head
down and focus.

Before the finals distractions can be severe. Your emotions are on over-
load because you actually have a shot at the dream. It may be the most important game of your competitive life. For many of you, your mind and
emotions are everywhere. Before finals is the most important time to keep
doing what you've been doing.

Above: East Chapel Hill player climbs the back of his Apex High School opponent. Photo source www.duke.edu

The bottom line is whatever preparation you've been doing, keep doing it. It's OK to accept congratulations from Grandpa and Grandma, but don't even think for one minute you're done. Humbly accept the congratulations, but inside stay serious—keep that Game Mode perspective. There is still a lot of work to do.

To maintain focus before finals, one of the key problems is dealing with your personal pent-up emotions, your teammate's pent-up emotions, the coach's pent-up emotions, and all of your peers bright, smiling, congratulatory faces. Everyone means well, but mostly it's pure distraction. Make sure that you keep your Game Mode mindset fully engaged. I'm not suggesting being intensely focused, I'm just saying don't emotionally celebrate. Use your Confidence Routines to keep your mind where it needs to be—focused on competing, not socializing and celebrating. Save that for after winning the Big game. Then it's party time!

By learning how to manage your emotions as you go through the transitions, you'll lessen the dramatic ups and downs from confident to doubtful. You'll learn how to win the composure battle. Once you master Big Dog Visualization, you'll be able to step-up and compete, with confidence. So show some teeth and let your Big Dog out!

S U M M A R Y

- Fight the confidence battle in the transitions.

- Focus your thinking on positive execution, not negative "what if" mental chatter.

- Be able to turn laser beam focus on and off.

- Effectively manage sideline dynamics.

- Be prepared; during the critical minutes is when your true competitive confidence will get tested.

- Stay calm. Control your emotions.

- Let your Big Dog out.

"The confidence battle is fought in the transitions, which is when most of us go nuts, meltdown emotionally and lose our composure. Stay away from negative "what if" mental chatter. Master Big Dog Visualization techniques, so you can step-up and compete, with confidence." — Steve Knight

Chapter 7

DREAM • Your Power

There's only one road to a state championship, and it's called d-e-d-i-c-a-t-i-o-n. The road of dedication is driven with discipline, and that's why many players fail—*lack of discipline is the giant killer.*

So many great athletes—young and old—never even come close to achieving their potential, because they refuse to discipline themselves.

Over the past few years my house has been full of teenagers; and after watching many of them grapple with issues of discipline, I will be the first to acknowledge, it's tough. In our communities today there are all too few living role models who are examples of true dedication and discipline. The majority of America's citizens have grown lazy and unmotivated.

"Dreams and dedication are a powerful combination."
— William Longgood

Above: Duke's Garnet Troy. Photo source dukenews.duke.edu

Left: Lakota East's Erik Reynolds celebrates a goal. Photo by Mike Simons

Discipline is almost non-existent in our schools, and the pleasure options teens have are extensive. The cars, cash, contraband, and girls are constant distractions from real achievement. Everyday, athletes are faced with the difficult decision of whether to work or pursue pleasure.

Let me say this: You'll progress rapidly if you're wise enough to realize that just because something is available, does not make it a good thing.

Did you get that point? When there is no party to go to, there is no decision to make, that's easy. But when you have options, *decisions* have to be made. And if you want to distinguish yourself from the average, you have to separate yourself from the pack, because the majority of your peers are *totally focused on entertainment and pleasure.*

Recently I received an email from Assistant Coach Blaine Davidson of the Bellevue High School Wolverines (Washington), and at the end of his message was the following quote, which is another way of expressing the point I'm trying to make: "The things that failures don't like to do are the very same things that you and I, including the successful, naturally like to do. We have to realize right from the start that success is something achieved by the minority, and is therefore unnatural and not to be achieved by following our natural likes and dislikes, nor by being guided by our natural preferences and prejudices." – Albert Gray

As that quote expresses so well, during your lifetime you won't see or meet very many people who are trying to achieve personal greatness. Why? It's too scary. The majority of people are mentally too weak to make courageous decisions.

As a teenager in America today, separating yourself from your peers to strive and excel, *is a courageous decision.*

At this point I think it's important that I tell you a little bit about myself, so if this chapter comes across too harsh, you'll understand why.

I would evaluate my athleticism as slightly above average, but am I physically gifted? No. Not in the least.

Physically, I was born a Little Dog.

My advantages are: 1) I love to practice; I truly enjoy working at getting better at something. When I retired from world-class competitive weight lifting after eleven years, I was looking for another sport to challenge myself with, and found golf. I hit two hundred balls - every day - until I achieved a three handicap. For me that wasn't a grind. That was fun. 2) I've never been highly social. I'm not antisocial, but hanging out and partying has never been compelling to me, even as a teenager. So from a training standpoint, I've never had to grapple with whether to work or play, train or party. I've always naturally gravitated towards work, not play. But, for many of you that battle is intense, and fought with extreme anxiety.

So, someone with my mindset looks at the work or play decision like, "What's your problem? Make the decision. Are you a champion or a slacker?"

As my youngest son Nick, who's eighteen, was reading the first draft of this chapter he shook his head and said, "Dad, you still don't get it. You're weird. Most of us don't think like you. For most of us, even if we have a real, tangible dream, forsaking our friends and isolating ourselves to train is like solitary confinement. *It's not a simple decision.*"

Many of your coaches, especially those who know how to win, will come across with a similar black and white mindset; either you do or you don't. Now, for the first time I realize clearly that for a lot of you, you get stuck in the middle; pulled in both directions.

So how do I help you find the motivation and discipline to party and socialize less, and work and train more?

Above: Players unknown. Nebraska Wesleyan Men's Soccer. Photo source: nebrwesleyan.edu

Here's the bottom line: as an athlete, especially at the high school level, you can't have it all. An athlete's commitments are triple those of most non-athletes. Like it or not, if you really want to excel, there isn't enough time to do it all. The main reason is sleep. For athletes, rest is critical. You train and practice hard; you lift weights and condition. The only way to recover and regenerate is consistent sleep. Partying and "hang-time" cut into sleep. Why? Because you have to get up at six or seven in the morning to get to

school, or even earlier to workout before school, while all of your party buddies are snuggled-in, warm, snoring in their beds. They have nothing to get
up for other than the next party. *You have a dream.*

Clutch Play: *Tackling certainly requires physical ability and skill. But it
requires even more discipline. Late in the game, after fighting for position
for 40 minutes fatigue, can overcome even tireless competitors. Why? Because fighting for position is about dedication and discipline—the desire to
own the ball. If you want to be a "clutch" player, you have to need the ball;
you have to focus on never letting it out of your sight. Ask yourself: Do you
want the ball bad enough to chase it like it's your last meal? Do you have
the mental power to tear through your opponents who want it just as badly
as you do? To have more success, you have to play harder and with more
power than the other guys on the filed. Physically, that takes dedication to
conditioning, strength training, and giving it your all at practice. But that
isn't enough. Being a clutch player takes dedication to mental discipline as
well. So during the week off the field, work hard and stay focused, develop
the mental discipline of a competitor who needs to own the ball. Your dedication and mental discipline off the field will translate into more intense
performance on the field. To be a champion, to rise above the average, takes
mental focus, dedication, discipline, and sacrifice. If you want it bad
enough, discipline yourself to get it.*

So, if you struggle with discipline how do you get some?

First, let's look at the definition in the dictionary: "**dis-ci-pline**: activity,
exercise, or regimen that develops or improves a skill."

As I'm sure you already know, discipline is not about fun, it's about
work.

Becoming genuinely disciplined is difficult; the only way I know how to
become disciplined is to have a *real dream.* You must clearly understand
why you're doing what you're doing, why it's important, and why nothing
is going to get in your way to achieve your dream … *absolutely nothing.*

Daily Schedule

Champion	——————▶	Slacker
6:15	30 minute run.	Sleep
7:15	Food	Still sleeping
7:50	School	Still sleeping—skip school
12:30	Food	Food
1:10	Weight Training Class	Smoke dope
2:50	Practice	Video games
5:30	Food	Food
6:00	Home work.	Smoke more dope.
7:00	Hang-out	Hang-out
9:45	Visualization Training	Hang-out
10:00	Lights Out	Party Time

Outcome: State champion. Solid work ethic. College. Great job. A future.

Outcome: Drop-out. Lifetime of addiction, and constant pursuit of pleasure.

When creating your dream, it's very important to understand the difference between your dream and your goals. Your dream is not a goal. Whereas, in visualizing, I advised you not to focus on the rewards, but to focus on the battle; your dream is the opposite; it's all about the rewards. Your dream is what you're going to obtain emotionally from all your dedication, discipline, and hard work.

Too often, we only focus on goals, which tend to be bland and tasteless. Your dream is where you find and feel the emotion and the glory. Goals are short term "markers" on the way forward to accomplishing your dream.

This is where most of you get lost; you don't create a vision for yourself. Think, gentlemen. Picture the future, not just short-term pursuit of pleasure.

Wanting to be a state champion is a goal, not a dream. All those things you'll get from winning the state title, those things are the dream.

Example: At that time in your life when you wanted your first car, bad, why was that desire so intense? Because you had a variety of mental pictures of what it would be like to have a car: feeling cool, being free, dating, and running around with your buddies. You had all sorts of feelings that went along with having a car. *That's a dream.*

Working toward a championship has to have the same feelings and meanings, or there's no motivation. Are you seeing it?

Recently, I was talking with an old weightlifting buddy Rick Mooney, in North Carolina. Since we're proud dads, of course, we talked mostly about our sons.

His son Will is going to be a high school senior this year, and is a baseball fanatic. If Will can play year-round, he does. He works diligently and

Above: Marco Velez rips off his jersey in celebration of the match-winning goal over Portland at Seahawks Stadium. Photo source: soundercentral.com

consistently at improving his game. He's already getting letters-of-interest from top colleges. I asked Rick if Will had his sights on the Pros. Rick belly laughed and said, "He lives, eats, and breathes the Pros."

Without even asking Will specifics, I know he has a vision of what it will be like to be in the Pros: catching the big game, throwing a key runner out at second base, maybe even signing the big contract, or blasting a homer to win the series.

It doesn't matter. Whatever Will's specific dreams are, he has feelings and emotions associated with his dreams. They are very real and they drive him forward. Will sets short-term goals to improve his performance; as he improves, the goals change. But the dream stays the same.

Your Power

Your dream is your power. Ask yourself: Why are you out for soccer? Why put yourself through the tough practices, training, and hard work? Why do you want to be a champion? What's your dream?

So many of you vacillate between being great, and being a contender. Some days you're on, and some days you're off. Some days you have the dream, but most days you don't. OK, yeah, it's fun to party, but what are you really getting out of it other than immediate gratification? Answer: nothing.

I can only hope that I'm expressing this point with perfect clarity, *so you get it*. To be able to say "no thanks" to the social opportunities that present themselves everyday, all day long, and instead go train or prepare, requires a dream. The clarity of your dream is what helps you stay dedicated. If you don't have a real dream driving your desire to excel, and if those reasons aren't *crystal clear*, staying committed will be a tremendous challenge, if you can stay committed at all.

Your dream is your emotional power.

Weak *no-dream* examples: 1. "I don't know; it's something to do." 2. Your friends want you on the team. 3. Your dad played soccer. 4. Coach says: "You could be a great soccer player."

Strong *big-dream* examples: 1. Your future is college and you need a scholarship. 2. You want to see how far you can push yourself. 3. You want to prove to yourself and everyone else that you can be great at something. 4. You want to distinguish yourself in our community as an individual who can achieve. 5. Best of all, "you" want to be a champion.

There are many other examples of weak and strong dreams. It is absolutely vital that you have a clear, strong vision of *your dream*, and yes, everyday it will be a battle—options require making decisions. Again, most Americans have too many pleasure options, and they don't make courageous decisions that forsake immediate pleasures for long-term achievements.

Here's where you might be thinking, "I have my dream, but I still struggle with dedication and discipline." I know many of you feel that way.

Sacrifice

The conflict is that many of you have not embraced, grasped, or taken hold of the *fact* that dedication and discipline mean sacrifice. This isn't a lecture; it's reality.

In order to be a champion at anything, you have to do things which elevate yourself above the average; that requires sacrifice. "**sac-ri-fice**: the surrender or destruction of something valued for the sake of something having a higher or more pressing claim."

Translation: Less party, more work, equals Big Dog status.

Going back to my perspective. I never really had to sacrifice in order to achieve. I didn't really care about partying and socializing. So for me it wasn't a big deal, so no big sacrifice.

For most of you it's a HUGE deal. I have to say, I feel for you. But the reality is, if you're going to excel **you have to submit.** You have to submit yourself to the reality of striving for excellence. You have to realize the bottom line - you can't have it all. That's just the way it is. As kids, we kick and scream over that reality, not realizing that it's the difference between becoming a champion and staying a contender. A champion will submit himself to the sacrifices of training and the pursuit of a higher dream, realizing that in order to acquire the reality of his dream, sacrifices have to be made.

Personal story: Recently I was involved with a high school senior who is a gifted athlete, *physically*. He played a variety of sports since he was a puppy. Football and basketball ended up being his two primary interests.

When he got to high school he was heading down the party road, and by his sophomore year he was pretty much self-destructing. His junior year was a disaster; academically he was a no-show, and, of course, he was not eligible.

He had been a good friend of my son Nick for years. The summer before his senior year we ran into him. After sharing his personal story, we offered to take him in, hoping that a fresh start and new environment would help him get back on track to finish high school, and ultimately go to college.

Right: Williston Northampton goalkeeper Mickey Meyer reaches for the ball as Wilbraham & Monson midfielder Adam Palencia moves in. Wilbraham won, 3-2. Photo by David Molnar/Union-News

"If you find a path with no obstacles, it probably doesn't lead anywhere."

— Frank A. Clark

At first, he was negative and reluctant. He thought he was too far behind, besides, there was no guarantee he would be eligible. I told him that *to assume* things in life is ... well ... ignorant, and suggested that with a couple of investigative phone calls he would know exactly what his options were. He agreed, and within a couple of calls we found out that he could enroll, and, he was eligible. He moved in with us, agreeing to my one condition; he had to go to school, no excuses. If he didn't, he'd have to move out.

He was pumped. He was back in school and on the football field again. Practice went great, and he quickly earned a starting position at corner. He contributed in the first couple of games and was looking forward to a great season. Then the phone call came.

I had kept what I thought was pretty close contact with him regarding his school attendance, and what I heard was, "Are you kidding, I'm going to every class. Why would I blow this?"

He lied. The Athletic Director told me he had been skipping class since the first day of school. His attendance record was barely 50%.

It was a sad day for me; unfortunately, I had to ask him to move out. I genuinely cared about this kid, and wanted to do all that I could for him. To keep up his end of the deal all that he had to do was go to class. There were no grade requirements. *Just go to class.*

As I was discussing with him why he chose to skip school, and blow the opportunity, he looked at me like I was some sort of idiot and said, "Because I want to have fun."

I'll never forget that, fun, at the expense of everything.

For whatever reason, it was more important for this young man to identify, connect with, and relate to kids who wanted to party, rather than the kids who wanted to excel. He made a decision, and now he has to live with it.

Trust me gentlemen, like it or not, dedication, discipline and sacrifice will have to be your best friend if you want to excel.

The Schedule

Once you decide, with *conviction*, that you can sacrifice certain social pleasures for a higher dream, and separate yourself from the "pleasure" pack, I strongly recommend that you put together a daily/weekly schedule to give yourself a framework to operate within. It can be as detailed as you like, which depends on your personality type. But, give yourself a daily/ weekly outline at what you *need* to do, along with what you *want* to do.

If you just take a little time to plan, you'll still be able to get some "hang-time" in, just not as much as your party friends. That's why you'll become a champion, and they won't.

It truly is your decision.

Training

This can be a short section. You know what your daily training chores are, so like Nike says, *"Just Do It."*

Above: Tottenville's Justin Scarpulla, left, and New Dorp's Aldo Garcia each try to head the ball. Garcia each try to head the ball. Photo by Hilton Flores/Staten Island Advance

The Test

Over the course of the season you'll be confronted many times with "do you" or "don't you" decisions. Do you get up and go to school, or sleep-in? Do you follow through with scheduled preparation, or blow-it-off and go hangout? Do you stay out late and party, or go home and rest up for tomorrow's training? *Each decision is a test.*

Your party "friends" will provide added pressure; "Come on man, just hangout." And of course, you'll want to, which isn't a bad thing; you're human. But each time you let partying cut into your training and preparation you're jeopardizing your potential for becoming a unique member of "our" championship community—those who can submit themselves to the sacrifices for higher achievements.

No doubt your decision record won't be perfect when the season is over. That's OK. I encourage you to make more positive decisions than negative. Make more decisions that will propel you towards your dream and success, rather than trap you among the average and failure.

Your dream is your power; it drives your *conviction* to do what is necessary, day in and day out, so you can step-up and compete with power and confidence. Remember: the road to being a champion is the road of dedication, discipline, and sacrifice. Dream and commit. Make positive decisions. Decide. Then do it!

110% Effort

Notice that I haven't even mentioned, "give it your all." Give everything you do 110% percent. Go, go, go, and go some more.

Intensity of effort is another deal. That comes from your personal drive, your Big Dog factor.

Personally, I would rather see young athletes give 90% effort, 100% of the time, rather than 110% effort, 80% of the time. The great champions of course give 200% effort, every single waking, breathing moment.

Dream Big

Without a vivid picture of a real dream, it doesn't matter who tries to push you, you won't have consistent motivation to make difficult social decisions, which absolutely jeopardize your chances of achieving success. Give yourself the opportunity to better yourself by creating a dream, and committing to the dedication, discipline, and sacrifice required.

Dream big and commit; it's your power.

S U M M A R Y

- Dedication leads to accomplishment.
- Make courageous decisions; separate yourself from the pleasure pack.
- Submit to the sacrifices of achievement.
- Everyday it's a battle; options demand decisions.
- Discipline yourself. Do what's required.
- Make choices to achieve your potential.
- Dream big. Create your power.

"I don't know of many instances when someone accomplished something of significance without first dreaming about it, and then committing to what was required to accomplish the task. I encourage all of you to dream, and commit." — Steve Knight

WinningSTATE-SOCCER
Program your mind. Win the confidence battle.

Championship
Interviews

5 nationally ranked state champion coaches and players share great advice, inspiring stories, and personal photos.

Special thanks to the coaches, players, and photographers.

Downers Grove South H. S.

Jon Stapleton, Head Coach • Downers Grove, IL

2004 Illinois AA State Champions

WSS: How important is individual confidence to a team's success?

STAPLETON: Obviously, confidence is critical in a lot of respects. You have to have the feeling that what you work on at practice is gonna to transfer over into a game situation. And I think a lot of that is confidence. If you feel comfortable in a practice setting; if you feel comfortable repeating a skill over and over again, then a lot of times that transfers into success on the playing field. Individual confidence is critical, especially in soccer, where you have 11 players trying to operate as a single unit. You have to feel comfortable and confident that you're not gonna let your teammates down, and that you're comfortable with your own play, and with your teammates play.

WSS: Have you seen exceptionally talented players, who, although they appear confident on practice field, are not confident in a game situation?

STAPLETON: I've definitely seen that. I don't know if it's due to the individual pressure they place on themselves or something else. You know, they must feel relaxed in practice; they're in a comfortable

Team Accomplishments:
- 2004 Regional Champions
- 2004 Sectional Champions
- 2004 State Champions—First time in school history
- 2004 Stats: 55/12/5

environment, in a comfortable setting, the pressure is not there, so when they're relaxed they go out and play. And boy, they look outstanding. But, once they get into a game situation; I don't know what it is, but some athletes have a hard time handling the pressure. It seems difficult for them to achieve the same comfort level in a game as they do in practice.

WSS: And at the same time, have you seen athletes who are not so gifted physically, but believe in themselves emotionally, and go out in game situation and perform beyond their physical capabilities?

Above: Downers Grove South H. S. boys soccer coach staff, (L-R): Unknown, Stapleton, Szmanski, and Mulder.

STAPLETON: Yeah, definitely.

WSS: As a coach, how do you help players build confidence, whether at practice or in game situations?

STAPLETON: In regards to practice situations, if you structure your practice in such a way that players know what to expect, then players know where you're coming from; to me that's an easy way to build individual confidence. For example: one thing that worked well for us, is posting a practice plan. When players arrive at practice, they know exactly what the expectation is, they know what drills they're gonna work on or things we're trying to focus their attention on. You might ask what does that have to do with a player's confidence?

Well, to me …. it's like in a classroom, you don't like to walk into the

> *"structure your practice in a way that players know what to expect,"*

room and not know what's going to be expected of you.

WSS: So, if you know a professor is organized and you know what's going on, and what to prepare for, you're more comfortable and confidence about what you're doing?

STAPLETON: Yeah, it's the same situation on the practice field. I lay out the practice plan and players immediately know what the practice is focused on; whether it's gonna be a physically strenuous practice or a mental type of practice, or a short session, or an intense practice. They know right from the start what to expect. And individually that's gotta help boost their comfort level and their confidence. They say, "You know what... I know what we're doing today and I'm prepared for it, I'm ready for it." There's no surprises. I've noticed as a classroom teacher that everybody learns in different ways. Some athletes thrive on being surprised, and some don't. This type of planning and preparation gives players some extra confidence by letting them know ahead of time what is going on. Another aspect of building confidence is treating players with respect. I mean, whether you're on the practice field or in a game situation, everybody's as competitive as you are; they all wanna win as much as you do. And sometimes mistakes are made. So, treating players with respect when they make mistakes, and helping them correct those mistakes in a positive manner helps

them stay confident. They need to know that I trust their abilities so they trust my abilities as a coach, which creates trust both ways and helps with positive reinforcement, which builds confidence.

WSS: Let's say one of your players didn't do so well in the first half of a game and you can see that they're struggling. What do you do when you see that they're confidence is not quiet where they it needs to be?

STAPLETON: I try to seek out those players and give them the individual attention they need. Something that I've done in a half time situation is help them mentally erase the first half and try to focus on the second half; what's coming up. As simple as that seems, it's not always as easy to get them to forget about previous mistakes. I also point out the things that worked well. If it's a player on our team is well known, and drawing a lot of attention, getting doubled teamed, and not able to execute at the level their accustomed to, and they get frustrated... I try to help them realize that due to their past success, they're drawing a lot of attention, which frees up other teammates to do other things. Statistically, they might be down in that particular game, but look what you're doing for everybody else. If a player in that situation is receptive to that, they can be positive and contribute a lot to the team.

WSS: That's really a good point. Part of what you just touched on is the core of our visualization program. You help

Above: Downers Grove South High School, Downers Grove, Illinois, 2004 AA boys soccer state championship team. Head Coach Jon Stapleton indicated that his assistant coaches and players should be very proud for winning the school's first state championship.

your players focus on their past success, which is exactly what we teach. Bring back those positive real experiences that were successful. We call it replacement visualization. The only way to get rid of negative thinking is to replace it with actual, real-time successful experiences. Also, that is a really important perspective for key players: you might not be having a great game personally, but look at what you're contributing to the team.

STAPLETON: Exactly. And ultimately a player has to be receptive and positive about that.

WSS: What if a player isn't that receptive?

STAPLETON: You know what, everyone is so individual. When you know a player who typically is not receptive to those types of things, as a coach, sometimes you want to shy away from doing something about it. But I have often looked back and said to myself that I probably should have taken more initiative and talked to that kind of a player more often. Maybe his body language is telling me that he's not hearing it, or doesn't want to hear it, but in reality he might be reaching out for connection, you know. So from my vantage point, one of the corrections I have made is to reflect on what I've done. So the next time, if I see a player like that I will approach him and try to get him a little bit more upbeat and try to help him see his success, that replacement thing you mentioned.

WSS: So some players are easier to talk to than others?

STAPLETON: It's kinda the same thing in the classroom; those students that don't show a lot of initiative and don't seem very receptive to you trying to connect with them and offering help, and you just think – "well, they don't want my help, so I'm gonna back off." But sometimes what they really want is for you to try a couple of times to earn their trust, and maybe from that point on they'll be more receptive. It's difficult, but I do my best to try more than just once or twice.

WSS: So what you're saying is if you're reading a player as closed, and not responsive, looking away and their body language is closed, don't let that dictate how you act. Use whatever skills you have to break through and get to that player—give it some extra effort.

STAPLETON: Exactly. And sometimes it really pays off.

WSS: Let's say a game has reached 5-minutes to go, and you're down a goal, and you know that one of your forwards is seriously lacking confidence at that specific moment; what do you do in that situation?

STAPLETON: Great question.

WSS: Do you ever pull them? To be able to communicate with them and stick 'em back in?

STAPLETON: I have definitely pulled players aside, pulled players out a game and tried to calm them down, but that kind of a decision would be on a very situational bases. One player comes to my mind: he was our top scorer this year; he probably scored 2 out of 3 of our team's points. Late in the game with 5 minutes to go, if he seems a little out-of-it, that's a kind of player that chances are I wouldn't pull out. Mainly because I think with him being on the field, if a ball bounces the right way and lands at his feet, he's the kind of kid that would react out of instinct and finish it. However, I would not hesitate if through the course of the game I noticed that a player is not performing or his mind is elsewhere. I wouldn't hesitate to put someone else in and try

> *"So next time, if I see a player like that I will approach him and try to get him a little bit more upbeat and try to help him see his success, that replacement thing you mentioned."*

Above: Two of the key players from the 2004 AA Illinois state champion Downers Grove South High School Mustangs.

to help the player figure out why he's so distracted or uncomfortable. So it's very situational. But like I said, if we're down one with 5 minutes to go, and a player with great history and track record is struggling, I would have a hard time pulling them, because in soccer you can't put him back in. I also coach basketball, and it's a totally different situation, you take them out, talk to them and boom, send him back in. But in soccer it's the nature of the game that I might be reluctant to do that, but definitely throughout the game I would not hesitate.

WSS: When you do pull a player to talk with them, what would you do?

STAPLETON: I never used the term replacement as you did before, but I think in my own terminology that is something I've used quiet a bit. I think that would be my focus. I pull them out, and again trying to build trust and building respect, a lot of times I give them a chance to speak – "hey, what do you see is happening out there? Give me some feedback." And let them talk a little bit. That shows that I do care about them, and trust their IQ when it comes to athletics.

WSS: So you don't start going off.

STAPLETON: Yeah, yeah. You know, "Where is your frustration coming from? What are you seeing?" And of course, most the time, they'll go off.

WSS: As they start explaining, that engages them as well, doesn't it?

STAPLETON: Yeah. It let's them speak first. Then, once I get their input, I'll say something like, "Relax a bit, let me tell you what I'm seeing. Let's see if we can work something out together to make this more successful." Number one, is treating them with respect, because you give them a chance to speak, and none of that "my way or the highway" type of thing. I'm a firm believer in that. I think we're in this together. Obviously there are some fundamental rules that as a coach you have to live by, and you decide. But it's important for them to be involved. That builds trust, that builds respect, and ultimately it gives them a chance to be open for communication to take place, and then from there you can kind of interject your voice, and hopefully between the two you come to a resolution.

WSS: Last question: what are the key elements to building a successful program?

STAPLETON: I think organization is the key.

WSS: What do you mean by that?

STAPLETON: If you're building a program, it extends beyond having a practice plan, because there are so many people involved in running your program. You're in charge of the freshmen, the sophomores, the varsity, and you have coaches appointed in all areas. And you want them to fit your model and what you're trying to get across, so the players kinda work their way up through the ranks and are prepared when they get to the varsity level. Plus you have to deal with parent issues and all kinds of things that have nothing to do with playing soccer. I think organization eliminates a lot of problems where they exist. So that's one of the keys in some respects, so everyone knows where they stand.

WSS: What are some of the specific things you do to organization the season?

STAPLETON: Number one, we do "meet the team night" at the beginning of the year, where go over the expectations for the entire program. We give opportunity for parents to ask questions, and really kinda clear the air from the start. Everyone knows what is expected. So that's kind of an organizational thing: the season is starting, you've made the team, and everyone knows where they stand. That's kinda step one. Second is putting together a schedule that extends beyond just the game schedule: here is the time schedule, here is the time frame your kids are expected to train in, and so forth. So then everyone kinda

Above: Team picture of the 2004 AA Illinois state champion Downers Grove South High School Mustangs.

knows how to plan accordingly; here is what I expect out of your kids; they're gonna be here from this time to this time, you know… and we stick to the schedule, if practice is over at 6:00, it's over at 6:00. And that builds confidence in our program. And as a coach, that holds you true to your word.

WSS: So first, you clearly have to know what you're doing.

STAPLETON: Right. That's the first key step. I'm a firm believer that teaching is coaching and coaching is teaching. So in class you have a timeframe, and need to be organized. Practice settings, game management, and the season in general are the same kinda thing. You

know: have you scouted an opponent? Do you know their weaknesses, their tendencies, and those kinds of things? Do your players know them? An important part of coaching is to convey those things to your players ahead of time. I think that helps build confidence. Just knowing who we're gonna deal with as a team, the basic tendencies of our opponents gives us a game plan, which helps us focus as a team. So to me, those are some of the tangible things that go a long way.

Camp Verde High School

Dave Miller, Head Coach • Camp Verde, AZ

2004 Arizona AAA State Champions

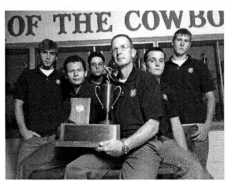

WSS: What was your background in soccer before you started coaching?

MILLER: I was a soccer dad. My children came up in the AYS soccer program, and then we went from that to clubs. As they became older and started playing in high school, I followed them around as an involved parent. I started attending coaching clinics, and then had an opportunity to coach club. Then I went from club coaching to being a JV coach for 5 years, and when an opening for a varsity coach came up, I took the position.

WSS: Quiet a progression.

MILLER: Yeah, but it probably would have been a bit easier if I had actually played the sport.

WSS: Yeah, that was my next question. You didn't play?

MILLER: No. You don't have to know the sport to be a good coach. I think coaching is about putting players in the right position at the right time to be successful. You do a lot of evaluation of skills and opportunities. I have a great training staff that

Team Accomplishments:

- 2004 3A Arizona State Soccer Champions
- State semi-finals 4 years in a row
- Coach Miller - Coach of the year last 3 years

I brought along with me. Ex-players that came back to be in the program, to demonstrate and teach skills and to mentor the young men as they go through our program. And what I do is probably…you know, I know what I want, I know the style of play, and that's what we do.

WSS: What do you mean style of play?

MILLER: I think that's the most important thing. One thing that confuses a lot of young players is not knowing what's expected of them. At the very beginning of the season,

Above: 2004 Arizona 3A state champion Camp Verde Cowboys.

Left: (L-R) Seth McCabe, Isaac Orellanand, Zach Davis, Coach Miller, Trevor Hammond, and Andy Brooks. Photos by Jared Dort/Verde Valley News

when you're still in pre-season, you have a style of play that you use. You establish that style by looking at the skill level of the players you have coming in, the experience level, and what they need to do to be successful. And you adapt and develop the style that gives them the best opportunity to succeed. If you have a lot of players with good ball control, you make sure your style of play accentuates that. If you have people who might not have good ball control, but can send the ball and play real physical, then you develop a physical game.

Each team, each year, is different. And that's what you do as a head coach; evaluate your players and their character and experience and develop a style of play that is gonna help them to be successful throughout the year. And for the team to succeed, you have to establish that style of play early, make sure they understand their role in that style, and then coach during

"adapt and develop the style that gives them the best opportunity to succeed,"

practice and allow players to play during the game. Too many coaches try to do too much coaching during the game, when that coaching should have been done during the practice session. As far as player development goes, there are very few things you'll be able to say or do in order to affect a change during the middle of the game.

WSS: We hear this from coaches all the time, that each season is a new season. And they didn't try to jam a particular style into the new group of guys that they get each year. They really adopt.

MILLER: You have to, in order to be successful. Currently, I have a lot of Hispanic players who brought their own flavor to the game. They're passionate for game, but not as disciplined as some of the other players. So we had to adapt and change our style of play for that, but still having them play within the system. And it's been good for them, it allowed them to be more involved in the school, and feel a sense of school pride that they possibly didn't have beforehand. And a lot of Hispanic players, since they've immigrated to the US, don't have that same broad family support, so we try and do that with our pre-season program, summer training, and give them a forum to play. And then they get a chance to come in and meld with the team, and it's been great. One thing I love about my teams over the last 4 years is the ethnic diversity, the diverse family that developed within the team itself.

WSS: Can you distinguish a confident player from a non-confident player?

MILLER: I think so... by the way they carry themselves. In soccer you have so many opportunities to succeed or to fail throughout the game. It's a lot of 1 vs. 1; there are 11 players on each team out there, but it still boils down to "are you better than the player from the other team who has the ball across from you?" If you're a confident player, you realize that you might have been just beaten, or had the ball taken away, or you tried to take the ball but were not successful, you can either hang your hand and stand there, or immediately get involved, you know – "give me another shot, give me another opportunity." Like the home-run hitter who gets struck out, the next trip to the plate he's still swinging away. It's the same thing in soccer. I look for young men like that, and put them in offensive positions. You know... in soccer, traditionally, there aren't many scores ... 3 nothing, 2 nothing, 2-2, so what you have to do is look for young man that might not have been successful on their last attempt, but are eager to give it another shot, because he knows that he's better, or feels that he's better, or feels that the team needs him to have that confidence.

WSS: What do you do for players with solid physical skills, but don't believe in themselves?

MILLER: You must leave the realm of coaching behind and become more of a mentor. Try to understand

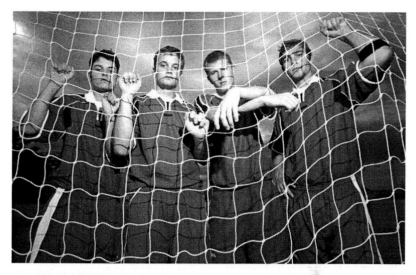

Above: (L-R) Seniors Zach Davis, Trevor Hammond, Andy Brooks and Seth McCabe. Photo by Jared Dort/Verde Valley News

what's driving that young man, and try to understand where he's coming from and what's going on in his life. Rather than trying to fit him into your mold, you have to search for a position that he can be successful in. Once you give them an opportunity to be successful, once they experience success, then they'll just go after it time and time and time again.

WSS: So success breeds confidence?

MILLER: That's exactly right. The skill of a coach is about putting young men and young people in positions to succeed. If you don't give a person an opportunity to succeed, then they will never know what it is, they will never develop confidence, because all they understand is failure.

WSS: So you do a lot of real-time analysis? You're assessing all of the time.

MILLER: You know, when I first started coaching, I spent a lot of time playing with the players, and being out there on the field as one of the players, participating in the drills and doing all those things. And then as I became more experienced, I realized that's not my job. My job is evaluation. During practice, it's my job to determine where I want the practice to go, the direction I want it to go, and the task I want to achieve. And then stand back and evaluate the players. How are they participating, where is the direction of the practice going. Do I need to change it or what do I need to do? If I want skill development, I put one of my assistant coaches with a player who needs to develop that skill. But then the evaluation of that player I do from the sidelines or at the end of practice when we do it together as a coaching staff. I think the reason a lot of coaches fail is they're out there trying to show the players that they can do the skill, instead of evaluating the players and planning out what they need to do. You need to get yourself back from the field a little bit, so you can evaluate. The whole purpose of coaching is to evaluate and to make adjustments.

WSS: So rather than pumping them up, and talking about confidence, put them in situations where they can be confident, taste it, and then want to go after it.

MILLER: Exactly. Tailor a game or a practice situation where the young men can experience success, that's what's important. Once they understand how to kick the ball straight, and they've been kicking it crooked for the whole season, and you can make an adjustment in the way they address the ball, the way they attack the ball, and then see the success, they'll be anxious to get back out there and do it again, again, and again.

WSS: Because nobody wants to fail.

MILLER: That's the whole point. Nobody wants to fail. Young people want to succeed. And they want you to show them how, to put them in situations so they can succeed.

> *That's the whole point. Nobody wants to fail. Young people want to succeed. And they what you to show them how, to put them in situations so they can succeed.*

WSS: You're playing in a critical game, and you're coming down to the final minutes, how do you handle your team?

MILLER: First, I think that the coach has to be confident. I mean we've all seen the coaches who are raving up and down the sidelines, yelling and griping about every call. And as a young coach, I probably was one of those types of coaches. Then I went to a coaching clinic and the person putting on the clinic said – "if you're not satisfied with the attitude of your team, before you get upset, look at yourself. How are you carrying yourself on the sidelines? What are you doing? What is your attitude? And then, if it isn't exactly what you want, there is the problem." And that was it. I looked at myself introspectively, and saw that the team was reflecting me. When they're all upset and getting cards,

**Above: Andy Brooks (right) celebrates with Seth McCabe (5).
Photo by Jared Dort/Verde Valley News**

and doing whatever they were doing, that was me. I mean, I was on the sidelines challenging every call, and was upset about everything. That was probably the biggest personal change in my coaching carrier.

So about 9 years ago, when I was still coaching clubs, it just hit home. I went out the next season and decided what I was gonna do – I was gonna show strength and control on the sidelines. Then your players do

the same thing. They're looking for a leader on the sidelines, rather than somebody there fanning the flames and trying to divert responsibility. I was one of the coaches who were always like – "if you really wanted to win, you would do this and that." I mean, if they didn't want to win they wouldn't be out there. I really had to change my thinking and my approach. They want to win, they want to try hard, and they want to be successful. So why ask them stupid questions? Give them positive input when they're out there. And I think, with young men, when I meet with them during the game or during the halftime situation, I try to limit it to about a 3-4 minute talk. That's about the attention span that they have during that time. So realize the attention span of the player,

be sharp, have your points, make them relevant, and then allow them to make the adjustment.

WSS: In soccer, when it's coming down to the last key plays do you talk to your players eye to eye?

MILLER: Since it's a fluid game and there are no timeouts, if there is something I need to do, I'll substitute a player, as long as the American game allows free substitution. I'll pull a player off the field, give them specific direction, and reinsert them into the situation. Here in Camp Verde we're called the Camp Verde Cowboys. And we have a thing when it's the last 15 minutes of the game we call it Cowboy Time. At that point everybody on the team knows that it's time to gear up. We turn the intensity up. Whether we're

Above: Senior Seth McCabe. Photos by Jared Dort courtesy of Verde Valley News

Left: Defensive specialist Alfonso Pesquiera (left).

ahead or behind, it's Cowboy Time. We didn't loose a game at home this year, and we try to defend the home turf really strong. And during a couple of games when we were behind or tied, it's usually the guys on the bench who remind everybody what time it is. And that sort of inspires guys on the field to turn it up. The team I had this year was probably not my most talented team over the last 4 years, but it was probably my best team. We understand what the team concept is, that you don't play only for yourself, but for everybody else who's on the team with you. And we had players throughout the season who would step-up and carry the team from time to time. And that's all good, that's all special, and that's the reason I coach. That's still the pure aspect of the sport: they're playing for the team, they're playing for the love of the game.

Note: Special thanks to Jared Dort of Verde Valley News for his great photos. Thanks Jared!

Stephen Bickford
Green Hope High School • Cary, NC

2004 NSCAA Adidas National Player of the Year

Stephen Bickford
Green Hope High School
Cary, North Carolina

Senior: 04 season
Height: 5'11"
Weight: 140 lbs.
40: 4.35

WSS: How do you maintain confidence in pressure situations?

BICKFORD: I guess knowing what you're capable of is the most important thing. And being realistic with yourself; knowing your limits and knowing your strengths as well.

WSS: Since everyone has different strengths and weaknesses, how do you define those for yourself?

BICKFORD: For physical strength – you have to know whether you can use your speed, if you have speed. Or, if you're not a very fast player, but you're really strong on the ball, then you need to adjust your play based on what's gonna work for you.

WSS: So if someone is studying a better player who has great speed, if you don't, you gotta adjust.

BICKFORD: Exactly. Study better players who play your type of game. It will make more sense because you can see it working for you.

Forward

Career Highlights:

- 2004 NSCAA/Adidas National Player of the year
- 2004 NC Athlete of the Year
- MVP Adidas ESP Summer Camp
- National Team member

Above: Bickford blows past a defender.

Left: Bickford receives the North Carolina Athlete of the year award from Adam Gold, a local radio personality.

WSS: As a forward, how would you classify your strengths?

BICKFORD: I would say my strengths are my speed and my timing.

WSS: What do you mean by timing?

BICKFORD: Knowing the right time to make a run into a space, to check or check away from the ball, get out wide and try to find a channel, that sort of thing.

WSS: So you've got good field vision?

BICKFORD: Right.

WSS: What about your weaknesses?

BICKFORD: Strength is probably my biggest weakness; I'm not a very big person.

WSS: So that's why you're in the weight room?

BICKFORD: Yep.

WSS: In a situation when you're feeling the pressure, how do you deal with yourself when your confidence is sort of lacking a little?

BICKFORD: That usually isn't the problem for me; I'm very confident in my abilities. Some people might say – "oh, he's cocky," or something like that, but I really don't see myself as cocky. I know what I can do and I just use that to my advantage, knowing that I can make things happen.

WSS: Interesting. Why don't you doubt yourself?

BICKFORD: Because of past experience. I had successes in the past, and I just keep trying to build on that.

WSS: Good point.

BICKFORD: I know that I've succeeded, I know that I can continue to succeed if I keep doing what I've been doing and if I keep trying to improve myself.

WSS: What happens when you get in a real high-pressure situation, you know the ball is coming your way, and you've gotta do something? What's your mental process? What are you thinking about?

BICKFORD: That's a tough question. What am I thinking about? Usually it's scoring…pretty much. When I get the ball and say to myself – "Alright. You've gotta do this." But if a better opportunity opens up for somebody else, I'll dish

it off to them just as fast. I try to do whatever I can do in order for our team to get results.

WSS: You're thinking all the time?

BICKFORD: Yep, pretty much. You have to.

WSS: During pressure situations, you're not mentally going through the – "What if I don't? What if I can't?" You don't go through negative thinking?

BICKFORD: You really can't ever think about the negative, if you expect to succeed.

WSS: "What if I miss? What if I can't handle it? What if this guy stuffs me?"

BICKFORD: If you think like that, more likely than not, you will fail. You can never anticipate failure.

WSS: Let's go back in time… how long have you been playing?

BICKFORD: Since I was 4 years old.

WSS: So you've been playing forever. Have you always been confident, not negative? Or were there times when you would get in to that "Oh my gosh, what if?" negative thinking?

BICKFORD: The only time I've ever felt like that was whenever I moved to a new team. Because I always wanted to make an impact right when I got there, whichever team I was playing for. But that was only fleeting thoughts maybe. I didn't give it too much time, I just kinda said to myself – "No, you'll be fine, don't worry about it."

WSS: "What happens if I can't perform? What happens if I don't measure up?"

Above: NSCAA 2004 player of the year Stephen Bickford focuses on keeping the ball in play.

BICKFORD: Right. And then I'll just say – "Relax. You know you're gonna do great."

WSS: Do you have a lot of positive support around you?

BICKFORD: Absolutely: coaches, teammates, family, everybody has just been awesome.

WSS: Positive support really helps?

BICKFORD: Yeah, definitely.

WSS: What advice do you give middle-schoolers and freshman who are looking to you as a role model, what do you tell them? What's important?

BICKFORD: It really depends on the player, the type of player they are, the position they play, and their style of play. I actually do a lot of camps, so I get to work with kids like that a lot, which is really fun. But you know the thing I stress most is confidence. You have to know that you'll succeed.

WSS: So you gotta believe it, not just think it, but believe it in your heart.

BICKFORD: Right. If you don't believe it, it won't happen.

WSS: If someone doesn't' believe down deep, how do they get there?

BICKFORD: You just have to relive your positive experiences, and the times you thrived and were really successful.

WSS: You're talking our language – we call it *replacement*. You can't just sit there and say – "I'm gonna do good, I'm gonna do good." You have to mentally relive your successful experiences so you can really feel them and believe you can do it again.

BICKFORD: Exactly.

WSS: Did anybody teach you that? Or did you naturally sort of do that?

BICKFORD: I've kinda always done that. At camps they stress visual imaging; visualizing success before you play; what you're gonna do and stuff like that.

WSS: But it sounds like you've added a twist; it's not just imagining and envisioning success; you're actually reliving successful moments.

BICKFORD: Right.

WSS: Which we suggest is a serious difference, because your mind can believe in those real experiences more than imagining what "might" happen.

"What I do before every game is sit down and just think about all goals that I've scored in the past, all different kinds: headers, left footed, right footed, volleys, ..."

BICKFORD: Yeah. Right. What I do before every game is sit down for about 5 minutes, close my eyes, and just think about goals that I've scored in the past, all different kinds: headers, left footed, right footed, volleys, beating players on the dribble, free kicks - everything. You have to relive all the stuff you have done, all those different ways that you've scored, because then you know – "I've already done this. I can certainly do it again."

WSS: Great job. I really encourage you to pass on that information about reliving actual successes vs. imagining success; it will really benefit younger players.

BICKFORD: Well, I hope so.

WSS: What else would you tell a young up-and-comer is important to succeed?

BICKFORD: Practice.

WSS: When you were an 8th or 9th grader, how much did you practice?

BICKFORD: Usually about an hour a day, 4 or 5 days a week.

WSS: Year around?

BICKFORD: Pretty much, unless the weather is bad, otherwise all the time.

WSS: Little breaks for vacations, but pretty much you're practicing 9 or 10 months a year?

BICKFORD: Actually, more than that, usually about 11 months out of the year. It's really important that kids get a rest too, so they're not practicing all the time. They forget that it's gotta be fun too.

WSS: So you have to keep it fun.
BICKFORD: It has to be fun.

WSS: How about nutrition?
BICKFORD: Nutrition is extremely important.

WSS: What is good nutrition?

BICKFORD: Usually the night before a game, I'll eat a good protein source and a good complex carbohydrate, some sort of pasta with chicken or something similar. And the day of the game, not anything too heavy but you still want something sort of like a peanut butter and jelly sandwich is great.

WSS: What is one of your most memorable moments during a game?

BICKFORD: Last summer I had 3 appearances for the U-18 National Team. I had a hat-trick with 20 minutes left. We were down a goal, but we won 3 to 1.

Michael Konicoff
Suffern High School • Montebello, NY

2004 NSCAA Adidas High School ALL-American

WSS: How important do you feel confidence is to your game?

KONICOFF: I think confidence is probably the most important thing in playing. That and also feeling comfortable. If you're not comfortable on the field your gonna have a real tough time playing.

WSS: And confidence is what will help you keep feeling comfortable?

KONICOFF: Exactly.

WSS: How do you maintain confidence?

KONICOFF: First of all, you can't be over-confident and feel that you're better than everyone else.

WSS: What happens if you do?

KONICOFF: You lose focus and control of the game, and may do things that you wouldn't normally do or try in a game. So you have to think that you're not necessarily better than everyone else, but just as good. I mean, you can't be afraid to try certain things, if you wanna go for it, go for it, but don't be overly confident.

Michael Konicoff
Suffern High School
Montebello, New York

Senior: 04 season
Height: 5'7"
Weight: 160 lbs.

Midfield

Career Highlights:
- 5 Years Olympic Development Team
- 2004 NSCAA/Adidas High School All-American
- U16 National Team Member
- U18 National Team Member
- Club Team 2X State Champs

Above: Michael Konicoff beats an opponent to the ball as soccer fans watch the action.

WSS: In terms of pressure-oriented situations, like if the guy you're up against is pretty formidable, and let's say you had a tough first half, what do you do in the second half to get things going?

KONICOFF: Personally, I like to get the ball. I feel like the more I have the ball in the game, the better I'll do. If I feel like my opponent is getting the best of me, I'll just try to get the ball more, get it on my feet, do a few simple things like move forward and dribble past the guy, or take a few shots. I think the more you have the ball, the more you get into the game, the more confident you become.

WSS: What is some of your self-talk? What do you say to yourself?

KONICOFF: I just say – "stay with it. Keep your head in the game." It's more of a mental thing than anything else. You just gotta keep talking to yourself positively and make sure you don't get negative and down on yourself.

WSS: What else do you to stay positive?

KONICOFF: I just keep a positive attitude and I don't give up. It can't be one of those things where you let down after the first half, when there is still another half to play. Whatever happened in the first half you gotta let it go, and focus on what's coming next.

WSS: Was your senior year a confident year?

KONICOFF: Yeah. It was great. I played with a great team, which really helps your confidence.

WSS: Let's go back when you were a freshman or even a middle-schooler. Can you remember times when you were doubtful? Or was there ever a time when you are doubtful?

KONICOFF: There were definitely times when I doubted myself.

WSS: What caused that?

KONICOFF: It can be few different things; in high school for instance, being a freshman you're gonna be smaller than a lot of the bigger guys; that my cause a lack of confidence.

WSS: So it might intimidate you a bit?

KONICOFF: Yeah, exactly. And then if things are not going your way for a game or two, it could bring you down a little bit.

WSS: What did you do to get your confidence back?

KONICOFF: You just gotta remember that a few bad games are not the end of the world. You've been down before, so you just gotta try to get back into it. You just gotta remember all of the times when it was going well.

WSS: When you say remember, what are you remembering?

KONICOFF: Well, part of my game preparation, like before the game or when I'm in a car, I like to think of the times when I scored a big goal or made a big play or something like that. This gives you that feeling like… you can do it again. So I like to do that before the game, just thinking of past times and remembering all the positive stuff. This gets all the negative thoughts out of your head.

WSS: So if things aren't going your way, you don't get negative?

KONICOFF: I might for a few seconds, right at that moment. But right after, I really try to get back to a positive mental place.

WSS: How you do that?

KONICOFF: Just thinking about it, focusing, and trying to forget that negative moment. You just gotta let it go.

WSS: So to get back to positive you bring back successful experiences from previous game situations?

KONICOFF: Yeah, exactly.

WSS: Lets talk about anger.

KONICOFF: It's in all sports: if you're down, you're gonna get angry. I think the best way to handle it is to not let it out, because you don't want to start flipping-out on the field, going off on the players, you know. I think if you can channel your anger, the best is to try and use

Above: Michael Konicoff focusing hard as he works the ball up the field.

it as a benefit, to play harder.

WSS: So you don't lose control?

KONICOFF: It has happened, but I really try not to. It's actually a waste of energy cause it sorta takes you out of your game.

WSS: Are you a water bottle thrower, bench kicker, throw your t-shirt kinda guy?

KONICOFF: No, none of that. Ever.

WSS: Cause some guys are, right?

KONICOFF: Yeah, there are definitely people like that, but that kind of behavior doesn't work for me.

WSS: I was talking with another nationally ranked player, and he was saying that if your opponents see you get angry, they target you. They'll know that they can frustrate you, and then they'll gang up on you and be all over you, to get you ticked, and get you off your game. Do you agree with that?

KONICOFF: Yeah. Especially with the trash talking you hear players doing all the time, if someone is doing that to you, trash talking, and you're focusing on what that player is saying, and then saying things back, and talking back – they're just gonna continue to do it, because they know it is frustrating you and getting you off your game.

WSS: So you don't even pay attention?

KONICOFF: Yeah, you just have to ignore it, to be able to play your game. To be able to do what you want to do, but sometimes it's hard

"Part of my game preparation ... when I'm in the car, I like to think of the times when I scored a big goal or made a big play or something like that. This gives you that feeling like... you can do it again."

to ignore it, but you just have to.

WSS: Do you ever work with kids? Do you work at camps and help the younger guys?

KONICOFF: I work at few camps over the summer. Not so much with little guys, but with middle schoolers and freshmen.

WSS: As someone who's done it and doing it, what do you tell the younger guys that want to play national level soccer?

KONICOFF: I just try and tell them to stay with the game. If you have a bad game, if you have a bad moment, you just gotta let go of it and move on. That one bad play or game should not affect what you do after that. You just have to stay confident and keep trying.

WSS: What's a unique part of your game?

KONICOFF: I'm a natural lefty. I think that plays a big part in my game.

WSS: Why, does that sort of throw guys off?

KONICOFF: Yeah, exactly. I play wide lift, so I can use the sidelines to my advantage, because my left foot is strong. I kinda have an easier time going out wide.

WSS: What about practice? Do you play all year?

KONICOFF: Yeah, I do. I play all of the time.

WSS: So you're practicing and playing 10-11 months a year?

KONICOFF: Yeah. You have to, to keep your skills sharp and your conditioning up.

WSS: So you're with the ball all the time?

KONICOFF: Yep, all the time.

WSS: Lift weights?

KONICOFF: Yep.

WSS: How important is nutrition?

KONICOFF: Real important. I think it's just as important as going out and practicing, lifting weights and running. I think it plays a huge factor in how well you play during games.

WSS: Give us some examples of good nutrition, or what's bad nutrition?

KONICOFF: You wanna try to stay away from all the junk food; the cakes, the candy, all that fattening stuff. I stick with good carbohydrates and protein.

WSS: So, good food, no fast food or soda pop, you don't eat much of that?

KONICOFF: I eat that occasionally, but not very often. I try to stay away from junk as much as possible.

WSS: Back to advising the young guys, how much do they have to practice?

KONICOFF: I say as much as possible, at least between 4 and 6 times a week, but if you can, you wanna try and do something every single day. It doesn't have to be much, just be with the ball for awhile each day and it makes a huge difference.

WSS: For how long? An hour or two a day?

KONICOFF: Just keep it going. You can't have 2 or 3 weeks go by when you're not doing anything.

WSS: Because your skills will drop?

KONICOFF: Definitely. Faster than you think. So I try and do something all of the time.

Note: A coach in Konicoff's home state said he's never seen anyone in New York, (Konicoff's home state), who can change the game as quickly as this rising star.

Chris Seitz
Thousands Oaks High School • San Luis Obispo, CA

2x Golden Glove at the National Championships

Chris Seitz
Thousand Oaks High School
San Luis Obispo, California

Junior: 04 Season
Height: 6'4"
Weight: 205 lbs.

WSS: How important is confidence in your game?

SEITZ: Confidence is defiantly important. If you don't have confidence you're more likely to fold-up under pressure. You have to have a back-up in your mind that you can do this, to get out there and do what you're expected to do.

WSS: What provides that? Why do some players have confidence and some don't?

SEITZ: It's the type of games that you play in, pretty much. Your gonna get nervous your first big game, but after you play in a couple you realize that there is no need to get nervous, you know that you're prepared and ready for what's gonna happen. The more games that you play that are important, the more confidence your gonna have going into them. Also, you just gotta relax and do what you know how to do.

WSS: What do you mentally before big games?

SEITZ: I was always taught to have that little mental picture in my head, but that only goes so far.

Goalkeeper

Career Highlights:
- Club Team 2X National Champions
- 2X Golden Glove at the National Championships
- Gatorade California High School Player of the Year
- U17 National Team Member
- All-American

WSS: What do you mean by that?

SEITZ: Whenever I went to camps they always said stuff like, "The

Above: Chris Seitz organizing the defense.

night before get a mental picture of yourself doing what you'll be doing the next day."

WSS: Like visualizing the future?

SEITZ: Yeah – visualizing and all that kind of stuff. I've done that and tried it a little bit, but for me it's mostly just being relaxed. Being relaxed and going out there and just doing the same things you've done in training.

WSS: How do you get relaxed?

SEITZ: Listening to music, I mean... different things work for different people.

WSS: Yeah, but what works for you?

SEITZ: I like to listen to music, personally.

WSS: Like headphones?

SEITZ: Yeah, definitely headphones.

Until the coach is ready to talk, I'm listening to music and thinking about what I have to do during the game.

WSS: Take us through that process before a big game.

SEITZ: I pretty much think about the big games I've been in the past, and things that I've done well in those games. I think about going out there and repeating everything I've done well in the past, and I keep thinking that through warm-ups.

WSS: Being a keeper, when there's only minutes left and the pressure is turned up, what do you do mentally?

SEITZ: It's pretty much like weathering the storm - doing what you can to stop the pressure. In practice you're always working on those last 2 minutes, and things that you can do to help out in those situations. It starts to come natural after a while. Like talking and organizing the defense and keeping them in the game, that's really important.

WSS: Meaning, you're providing a leadership position?

SEITZ: I mean, the keeper is supposed to be talking to his defense and organizing it and keeping them focused. So pretty much helping them out, I mean, the keeper is the eyes on the field, you can see the entire field in front of you, so you give your defense your point of view, talk to them, and try to organize them as best as possible.

WSS: What you mean by 'weather the storm' is when the ball is your score-zone, you just gotta weather whatever is gonna come your way?

SEITZ: Yeah, you just gotta do the best you can do slow it down as the time runs out.

WSS: From a mental standpoint, do you have any specific things that you do right then?

SEITZ: Just looking at my weak side and organizing the outside back. I don't really think that I need to relax or stuff like that.

WSS: You're thinking functional things.

SEITZ: I'm thinking more like my team needs to be organized, so the ball doesn't have to get near me, you know?

WSS: So pretty much you don't doubt yourself?

SEITZ: Well... I have confidence in my team. I have full confidence in the team I'm playing with, every time.

WSS: Period?

SEITZ: Well... yeah, pretty much.

WSS: Do you ever doubt yourself?

SEITZ: Not while I'm in the game. Like in practices and stuff, when I might be having a bad day. I mean there is always a certain amount of doubting that you'll have.

WSS: What kind of doubt?

SEITZ: Like – "should I be here,

Above: Chris Seitz looks downfield for an open slot.

should I be at this level, am I over-rated," stuff like, "do I belong here?"

WSS: You mean, "Can I live up to what's expected of me" kind of thing?

SEITZ: It's more like, "do I belong here with these people, this class of players?" Like when I was at the national team I questioned whether I belonged out there; I had to prove myself to myself everyday.

WSS: How do you handle that internal feeling of doubt?

SEITZ: Well, I tell myself that I do belong out there, and then go out there and prove to myself that I do belong there and that I can do whatever everyone else is doing around me. For instance, I went over to a Keeper's camp in England two years ago, there were a lot of different age groups there, all the way from professional teams down to 15-16 year olds like myself. I was probably the only guy with an American name out there, so the question, "do I belong out here?" came up a lot in my mind. By the end of the first day, because we weren't divided up into age groups, I was training mostly with 19-20 year olds. So I was always like – "do I belong in this age group?" But towards the end I told myself to just go out and do what I can to prove it.

WSS: What happened?

SEITZ: I mean I did fine. It was probably the best camp I've ever gone to, it's a straight goalkeeper camp; it got me in the best shape possible. I went right before the league started.

WSS: It made you elevate your game?

SEITZ: Yeah, definitely.

WSS: Some kids might have shrunk, doubted themselves, and hide in the corner.

SEITZ: I could have hid in the bushes or whatever and not gotten anything out of it.

WSS: But you wanted to go out there and see what you could do.

SEITZ: Yeah, just make the best of the situation. I mean, I came a day late to the camp, no one really knew who I was during my first training session, and I was shy towards people, but after a while I opened up and got after it.

WSS: It turned out good?

SEITZ: Yeah, the best camp ever.

WSS: How important is nutrition?

SEITZ: It's important. It's important to watch what you're eating while you're in the off season. Like for me right now, I can't play high school soccer because I transferred from another school, so it's important to stay fit on my own, and watching what I eat is a big part of that.

WSS: What's good nutrition?

SEITZ: Like salads over fast food. I wish I could say I do this all the time because it's not the easiest thing in the world. I mean, it's like when you're around town looking for a deli rather than something else.

WSS: What about soda?

SEITZ: I try to stick with lemonade and water.

WSS: What's breakfast like?

SEITZ: Right now, I'm not really eating breakfast because I have to wake up for a 7 o'clock class.

WSS: What's for lunch?

SEITZ: Subway or a deli sandwich, stuff like that.

WSS: What advice do you have for middle schoolers and freshman to be able to play at a national level?

SEITZ: Consistency. You have to be consistent with the easy stuff, because coaches don't want the keepers that do those fantastic saves but are not consistent with the easy stuff. But of course, occasionally, you'll need to make the big save that keeps your team in the game.

WSS: How do you work on consistency?

SEITZ: Practice, doing the same drills over and over again.

WSS: How much do you practice?

SEITZ: Right now I'm practicing every single day with my high school team, plus with my goalkeeper trainer, and sometimes on the weekends too. It sounds bad, but about 5-6 days a week.

WSS: How many months a year?

SEITZ: I don't really stop. Except vacations, I practice year-around.

WSS: So you're with the ball all the time?

SEITZ: Yeah, definitely. I haven't had even a half-month off so far. So practice is constant.

About the Author

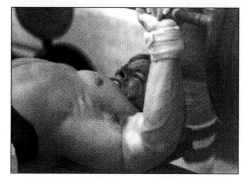

Photos by Kim Ross

A pioneer in the field of mental preparation for tournament competition, Steve Knight is a 4x State and 2x National Powerlifting champion, and current Oregon state record holder in the squat at 722 lbs.

Steve's breakthrough Big Dog Visualization techniques and confidence building routines transform doubtful, distracted athletes into focused, confident competitors. WinningSTATE Confidence Books are changing the way coaches and players mentally prepare for competition. The bottom line of Steve's teaching is: Confidence is a skill, not a genetic gift.

Steve resides in Portland, Oregon, is founder of Let's Win! Publishing; a devoted father to two grown sons; and is currently pursuing a degree at Portland State University.

ORDER THE BOOK

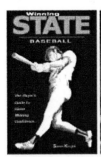 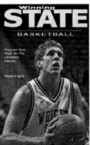  
  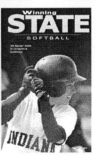